AF615182

William Cullen Bryant

The Riverside Literature Series

SELLA, THANATOPSIS
AND OTHER POEMS

BY

WILLIAM CULLEN BRYANT

WITH NOTES AND
A BIOGRAPHICAL SKETCH

BOSTON NEW YORK CHICAGO
HOUGHTON MIFFLIN COMPANY
The Riverside Press Cambridge

The Poems included in this number of the Riverside Literature Series are used by permission of Messrs. D. Appleton & Co., the authorized publishers of Bryant's Poems, and with the kind consent of Mr. Parke Godwin.

CONTENTS.

WILLIAM CULLEN BRYANT.

BIOGRAPHICAL SKETCH.

WILLIAM CULLEN BRYANT was born at Cummington, Massachusetts, November 3, 1794; he died in New York, June 12, 1878. His first poem, *The Embargo*, was published in Boston in 1809, and was written when he was but thirteen years old; his last poem, *Our Fellow Worshippers*, was published in 1878. His long life thus was a long career as a writer, and his first published poem prefigured the twofold character of his literary life, for while it was in poetic form it was more distinctly a political article. He showed very early a taste for poetry, and was encouraged to read and write verse by his father, Dr. Peter Bryant, a country physician of strong character and cultivated tastes. He was sent to Williams College in the fall of 1810, where he remained two terms, when he decided to leave and enter Yale College; but pecuniary troubles interfered with his plans, and he never completed his college course. He pursued his literary studies at home, then began the study of law and was admitted to the bar in 1815. Meantime he had been continuing to write, and during this period wrote with many corrections and changes the poem by which he is still perhaps best known, *Thanatopsis*. It was published in the *North American Review* for September, 1817, and the same periodical published a few months afterward his lines *To a Waterfowl*, one of the most characteristic and lovely of Bryant's poems. Literature divided his attention with law, but evidently had his heart. In 1821 he was invited to read a poem before the Phi Beta Kappa Society of Harvard College, and he read *The Ages*, a grave stately poem which shows his own poetic power, his familiarity with the great masters of literature, and his lofty, philosophic nature. Shortly after this he issued a small volume of poems, and his name began to be known as that of the first American who had written poetry that could take its place in universal literature. His own decided preference for literature, and the encouragement of friends, led to his abandonment of the law in 1825, and his removal to New York, where he undertook the associate editorship of *The New York Review and Athenæum Magazine.* Poetic genius is not caused or controlled by circumstance, but a purely literary life in a country not yet educated in literature was impossible to a man of no other means of support, and in a few months, after the *Review* had vainly tried to maintain life by a frequent change of name, Bryant accepted an appointment as assistant editor of the *Evening Post.* From 1826, then, until his death, Bryant was a journalist by profession. One effect of this change in his life was to eliminate from his poetry that political character which was displayed in his first published poem and had several times since shown itself. Thenceafter he threw into his journalistic occupation all those thoughts and experiences which made him by nature a patriot and political thinker; he reserved for poetry the calm reflection, love of nature, and purity of aspiration which made him a poet. His editorial writing was made strong and pure by his cultivated taste and lofty ideals, but he presented the rare combination of a poet who never sacrificed his love of high literature and his devotion to art, and of a publicist who retained a sound judgment and pursued the most practical ends.

His life outwardly was uneventful. He made four journeys to Europe, in 1834, 1845, 1852, 1857, and he made frequent tours in his own country. His observations on his travels were published in *Letters from a Traveller*, *Letters from the East*, and *Letters from Spain and other Countries*. He never held public office, except that in 1860 he was a presidential elector, but he was connected intimately with important movements in society, literature, and politics, and was repeatedly called upon to deliver addresses commemorative of eminent citizens, as of Washington Irving, and James Fenimore Cooper, and at the unveiling of the bust of Mazzini in the Central Park. His *Orations and Addresses* have been gathered into a volume.

The bulk of his poetry apart from his poetic translations is not considerable, and is made up almost wholly of short poems which are chiefly inspired by his love of nature. R. H. Dana in his preface to *The Idle Man* says: "I shall never forget with what feeling my friend Bryant some years ago [1] described to me the effect produced upon him by his meeting for the first time with Wordsworth's *Ballads*. He lived, when quite young, where but few works of poetry were to be had; at a period, too, when Pope was still the great idol of the Temple of Art. He said that upon opening Wordsworth a thousand springs seemed to gush up at once in his heart, and the face of nature of a sudden to change into a strange freshness and life."

This was the interpreting power of Wordsworth suddenly disclosing to Bryant, not the secrets of nature, but his own powers of perception and interpretation. Bryant is in no sense an imitator of Wordsworth, but a comparison of the two poets would be of great interest as showing how individually each pursued the same general poetic end. Wordsworth's *Three Years She Grew in Sun and Shower* and Bryant's *O Fairest of the Rural Maids* offer an admirable opportunity for disclosing the separate treatment of similar subjects. In Bryant's lines, musical and full of a gentle revery, the poet seems to go deeper and deeper into the forest, almost forgetful of the "fairest of the rural maids;" in Wordsworth's lines, with what simple yet profound feeling

[1] This was written in 1833.

the poet, after delicately disclosing the interchange of nature and human life, returns into those depths of human sympathy where nature must forever remain as a remote shadow.

Bryant translated many short poems from the Spanish, but his largest literary undertaking was the translation of the *Iliad* and *Odyssey* of Homer. He brought to this task great requisite powers, and if there is any failure it is in the absence of Homer's lightness and rapidity, qualities which the elasticity of the Greek language especially favored.

A pleasant touch of a simple humor appeared in some of his social addresses, and occasionally is found in his poems, as in *Robert of Lincoln.* Suggestions of personal experience will be read in such poems as *The Cloud on the Way*, *The Life that Is*, and in the half-autobiographic poem, *A Lifetime.*

The two poems which open this collection are the longest of Bryant's original poems, and, while as fairy tales distinct from the usual subjects which he has taken, present many of his characteristics.

Mr. Bryant's initials have been appended to such notes as are taken from the full collection of his poems; all other notes, whether introductory or foot notes, are the editor's.

SELLA.

[SELLA is the name given by the Vulgate to one of the wives of Lamech, mentioned in the fourth chapter of the Book of Genesis, and called Zillah in the common English version of the Bible. The meaning of the name is Shadow, and in choosing it the poet seems to have had no reference to the Biblical fact, but to the significance of the name, since he was telling of a creature who had the form without the substance of human kind. The story naturally suggests Fouqué's *Undine*, and is in some respects a complement to that lovely romance. Undine is a water-nymph without a soul, who gains one only by marrying a human being, and in marrying tastes of the sorrows of life. Sella is of the human race, gifted with a soul, but having a longing for life among the water-nymphs. That life withdraws her from the troubles and cares of the world, and she loses more and more her interest in them; when at last she is rudely cut off from sharing in the water-nymphs' life, is awakened as it were from a dream of beauty, she returns to the world after a brief struggle, mingles with it, and makes the knowledge gained among the water-nymphs minister to the needs of men.

The story must not be probed too ingeniously for its moral; it is an exquisite fairy tale, but like many of such tales it involves a gentle parable, which has been hinted at above. If a more explicit interpretation is desired, we may say that the passion for ideals, gradually withdrawing one from human sympathy, is made finally to ennoble and lift real life. The poet has not localized the poem nor given it a specific time, but left himself and the reader free by using the large terms of nature and human life, and referring the action to the early, formative period of the world. Observe Bryant's delicate and accurate transcriptions of faint characteristics of nature, as in lines 8, 12, 30, 35, 41, 215, 238, 389.]

HEAR now a legend of the days of old —
The days when there were goodly marvels yet,
When man to man gave willing faith, and loved
A tale the better that 't was wild and strange.
  Beside a pleasant dwelling ran a brook
Scudding along a narrow channel, paved
With green and yellow pebbles; yet full clear
Its waters were, and colorless and cool,
As fresh from granite rocks. A maiden oft
Stood at the open window, leaning out,
And listening to the sound the water made,
A sweet, eternal murmur, still the same,
And not the same; and oft, as spring came on,
She gathered violets from its fresh moist bank,
To place within her bower, and when the herbs
Of summer drooped beneath the mid-day sun,
She sat within the shade of a great rock,
Dreamily listening to the streamlet's song.
  Ripe were the maiden's years; her stature showed
Womanly beauty, and her clear, calm eye
Was bright with venturous spirit, yet her face
Was passionless, like those by sculptor graved
For niches in a temple. Lovers oft
Had wooed her, but she only laughed at love,
And wondered at the silly things they said.
'T was her delight to wander where wild vines
O'erhang the river's brim, to climb the path

11. Observe the various suggestions in the early lines of the poem of Sella's sympathy with water life.

Of woodland streamlet to its mountain springs,
To sit by gleaming wells and mark below
The image of the rushes on its edge,
And, deep beyond, the trailing clouds that slid
Across the fair blue space. No little fount
Stole forth from hanging rock, or in the side
Of hollow dell, or under roots of oak,
No rill came trickling, with a stripe of green,
Down the bare hill, that to this maiden's eyes
Was not familiar. Often did the banks
Of river or of sylvan lakelet hear
The dip of oars with which the maiden rowed
Her shallop, pushing ever from the prow
A crowd of long, light ripples toward the shore.
  Two brothers had the maiden, and she thought,
Within herself: "I would I were like them;
For then I might go forth alone, to trace
The mighty rivers downward to the sea,
And upward to the brooks that, through the year,
Prattle to the cool valleys. I would know
What races drink their waters; how their chiefs
Bear rule, and how men worship there, and how
They build, and to what quaint device they frame,
Where sea and river meet, their stately ships;
What flowers are in their gardens, and what trees
Bear fruit within their orchards; in what garb
Their bowmen meet on holidays, and how
Their maidens bind the waist and braid the hair.
Here, on these hills, my father's house o'erlooks
Broad pastures grazed by flocks and herds, but there
I hear they sprinkle the great plains with corn

31. The clouds which she sees deep beyond are of course the reflection of the clouds passing over the well, as it is not the rushes but the image of the rushes which she sees in the water.

And watch its springing up, and when the green
Is changed to gold, they cut the stems and bring
The harvest in, and give the nations bread.
And there they hew the quarry into shafts,
And pile up glorious temples from the rock,
And chisel the rude stones to shapes of men.
All this I pine to see, and would have seen,
But that I am a woman, long ago."
 Thus in her wanderings did the maiden dream,
Until, at length, one morn in early spring,
When all the glistening fields lay white with frost,
She came half breathless where her mother sat:
"See, mother dear," said she, "what I have found,
Upon our rivulet's bank; two slippers, white
As the mid-winter snow, and spangled o'er
With twinkling points, like stars, and on the edge
My name is wrought in silver; read, I pray,
Sella, the name thy mother, now in heaven,
Gave at my birth; and sure, they fit my feet!"
"A dainty pair," the prudent matron said,
"But thine they are not. We must lay them by
For those whose careless hands have left them here;
Or haply they were placed beside the brook
To be a snare. I cannot see thy name

72. The reader will recall instances of the magical or transforming character of slippers and the like: Mercury with his winged sandals, Cinderella with her glass slippers, the seven leagued boots, Puss in boots. A covering for the head is connected with the power of command and the power of invisibility: a covering for the foot with magical power of motion.

82. In the mother's inability to read Sella's name on the slipper is suggested that unimaginative nature which is so often represented in fairy tales for a foil to the imagination. Hawthorne has used this open-eyed blindness with excellent effect in his story of the *Snow Image*.

Upon the border, — only characters
Of mystic look and dim are there, like signs
Of some strange art; nay, daughter, wear them not."
Then Sella hung the slippers in the porch
Of that broad rustic lodge, and all who passed
Admired their fair contexture, but none knew
Who left them by the brook. And now, at length,
May, with her flowers and singing birds, had gone,
And on bright streams and into deep wells shone
The high, mid-summer sun. One day, at noon,
Sella was missed from the accustomed meal.
They sought her in her favorite haunts, they looked
By the great rock, and far along the stream,
And shouted in the sounding woods her name.
Night came, and forth the sorrowing household went
With torches over the wide pasture-grounds
To pool and thicket, marsh and briery dell,
And solitary valley far away.
The morning came, and Sella was not found.
The sun climbed high; they sought her still; the noon,
The hot and silent noon, heard Sella's name,
Uttered with a despairing cry, to wastes
O'er which the eagle hovered. As the sun
Stooped toward the amber west to bring the close
Of that sad second day, and, with red eyes,
The mother sat within her home alone,
Sella was at her side. A shriek of joy
Broke the sad silence; glad, warm tears were shed,
And words of gladness uttered. "Oh, forgive,"
The maiden said, "that I could e'er forget
Thy wishes for a moment. I just tried
The slippers on, amazed to see them shaped

So fairly to my feet, when, all at once,
I felt my steps upborne and hurried on
Almost as if with wings. A strange delight,
Blent with a thrill of fear, o'ermastered me,
And, ere I knew, my plashing steps were set
Within the rivulet's pebbly bed, and I
Was rushing down the current. By my side
Tripped one as beautiful as ever looked
From white clouds in a dream; and, as we ran,
She talked with musical voice and sweetly laughed.
Gayly we leaped the crag and swam the pool,
And swept with dimpling eddies round the rock,
And glided between shady meadow banks.
The streamlet, broadening as we went, became
A swelling river, and we shot along
By stately towns, and under leaning masts
Of gallant barks, nor lingered by the shore
Of blooming gardens; onward, onward still,
The same strong impulse bore me till, at last,
We entered the great deep, and passed below
His billows, into boundless spaces, lit
With a green sunshine. Here were mighty groves
Far down the ocean valleys, and between
Lay what might seem fair meadows, softly tinged
With orange and with crimson. Here arose
Tall stems, that, rooted in the depths below,
Swung idly with the motions of the sea;
And here were shrubberies in whose mazy screen
The creatures of the deep made haunt. My friend
Named the strange growths, the pretty coralline,
The dulse with crimson leaves, and streaming far,
Sea-thong and sea-lace. Here the tangle spread
Its broad, thick fronds, with pleasant bowers beneath;
And oft we trod a waste of pearly sands,

Spotted with rosy shells, and thence looked in
At caverns of the sea whose rock-roofed halls
Lay in blue twilight. As we moved along,
The dwellers of the deep, in mighty herds,
Passed by us, reverently they passed us by,
Long trains of dolphins rolling through the brine,
Huge whales, that drew the waters after them,
A torrent stream, and hideous hammer-sharks,
Chasing their prey. I shuddered as they came;
Gently they turned aside and gave us room."
  Hereat broke in the mother, "Sella, dear,
This is a dream, the idlest, vainest dream."
  "Nay, mother, nay; behold this sea-green scarf,
Woven of such threads as never human hand
Twined from the distaff. She who led my way
Through the great waters bade me wear it home,
A token that my tale is true. 'And keep,'
She said, 'the slippers thou hast found, for thou,
When shod with them, shalt be like one of us,
With power to walk at will the ocean-floor,
Among its monstrous creatures, unafraid,
And feel no longing for the air of heaven
To fill thy lungs, and send the warm, red blood
Along thy veins. But thou shalt pass the hours
In dances with the sea-nymphs, or go forth,
To look into the mysteries of the abyss
Where never plummet reached. And thou shalt sleep
Thy weariness away on downy banks
Of sea-moss, where the pulses of the tide
Shall gently lift thy hair, or thou shalt float
On the soft currents that go forth and wind
From isle to isle, and wander through the sea.'
  "So spake my fellow-voyager, her words
Sounding like wavelets on a summer shore,

And then we stopped beside a hanging rock
With a smooth beach of white sands at its foot,
Where three fair creatures like herself were set
At their sea-banquet, crisp and juicy stalks,
Culled from the ocean's meadows, and the sweet
Midrib of pleasant leaves, and golden fruits,
Dropped from the trees that edge the southern isles,
And gathered on the waves. Kindly they prayed
That I would share their meal, and I partook
With eager appetite, for long had been
My journey, and I left the spot refreshed.
"And then we wandered off amid the groves
Of coral loftier than the growths of earth;
The mightiest cedar lifts no trunk like theirs,
So huge, so high, toward heaven, nor overhangs
Alleys and bowers so dim. We moved between
Pinnacles of black rock, which, from beneath,
Molten by inner fires, so said my guide,
Gushed long ago into the hissing brine,
That quenched and hardened them, and now they stand
Motionless in the currents of the sea
That part and flow around them. As we went,
We looked into the hollows of the abyss,
To which the never-resting waters sweep
The skeletons of sharks, the long white spines
Of narwhale and of dolphin, bones of men
Shipwrecked, and mighty ribs of foundered barks.
Down the blue pits we looked, and hastened on.
"But beautiful the fountains of the sea
Sprang upward from its bed; the silvery jets
Shot branching far into the azure brine,
And where they mingled with it, the great deep
Quivered and shook, as shakes the glimmering air

Above a furnace. So we wandered through
The mighty world of waters, till at length
I wearied of its wonders, and my heart
Began to yearn for my dear mountain home.
I prayed my gentle guide to lead me back
To the upper air. 'A glorious realm,' I said,
'Is this thou openest to me; but I stray
Bewildered in its vastness; these strange sights
And this strange light oppress me. I must see
The faces that I love, or I shall die.'
"She took my hand, and, darting through the waves,
Brought me to where the stream, by which we came,
Rushed into the main ocean. Then began
A slower journey upward. Wearily
We breasted the strong current, climbing through
The rapids tossing high their foam. The night
Came down, and, in the clear depth of a pool,
Edged with o'erhanging rock, we took our rest
Till morning; and I slept, and dreamed of home
And thee. A pleasant sight the morning showed;
The green fields of this upper world, the herds
That grazed the bank, the light on the red clouds,
The trees, with all their host of trembling leaves,
Lifting and lowering to the restless wind
Their branches. As I awoke I saw them all
From the clear stream; yet strangely was my heart
Parted between the watery world and this,
And as we journeyed upward, oft I thought
Of marvels I had seen, and stopped and turned,

224. How very often in fairy tales the human being has but to exercise the will to attain or to renounce the fairy power! It is only when one is under a spell, in the classic fairy tales, that the will is not recognized as the supreme authority.

And lingered, till I thought of thee again;
And then again I turned and clambered up
The rivulet's murmuring path, until we came
Beside this cottage door. There tenderly
My fair conductor kissed me, and I saw
Her face no more. I took the slippers off.
Oh! with what deep delight my lungs drew in
The air of heaven again, and with what joy
I felt my blood bound with its former glow;
And now I never leave thy side again."

So spoke the maiden Sella, with large tears
Standing in her mild eyes, and in the porch
Replaced the slippers. Autumn came and went;
The winter passed; another summer warmed
The quiet pools; another autumn tinged
The grape with red, yet while it hung unplucked,
The mother ere her time was carried forth
To sleep among the solitary hills.

A long still sadness settled on that home
Among the mountains. The stern father there
Wept with his children, and grew soft of heart,
And Sella, and the brothers twain, and one
Younger than they, a sister fair and shy,
Strewed the new grave with flowers, and round it set
Shrubs that all winter held their lively green.
Time passed; the grief with which their hearts were wrung
Waned to a gentle sorrow. Sella, now,
Was often absent from the patriarch's board;
The slippers hung no longer in the porch;
And sometimes after summer nights her couch

245. The humanizing of the character of Sella is effected by such touches as this.

Was found unpressed at dawn, and well they knew
That she was wandering with the race who make
Their dwelling in the waters. Oft her looks
Fixed on blank space, and oft the ill-suited word
Told that her thoughts were far away. In vain
Her brothers reasoned with her tenderly.
"Oh leave not thus thy kindred;" so they prayed:
"Dear Sella, now that she who gave us birth
Is in her grave, oh go not hence, to seek
Companions in that strange cold realm below,
For which God made not us nor thee, but stay
To be the grace and glory of our home."
She looked at them with those mild eyes and wept,
But said no word in answer, nor refrained
From those mysterious wanderings that filled
Their loving hearts with a perpetual pain.
And now the younger sister, fair and shy,
Had grown to early womanhood, and one
Who loved her well had wooed her for his bride,
And she had named the wedding day. The herd
Had given its fatlings for the marriage feast;
The roadside garden and the secret glen
Were rifled of their sweetest flowers to twine
The door posts, and to lie among the locks
Of maids, the wedding guests; and from the boughs
Of mountain orchards had the fairest fruit
Been plucked to glisten in the canisters.
Then, trooping over hill and valley, came
Matron and maid, grave men and smiling youths,
Like swallows gathering for their autumn flight.
In costumes of that simpler age they came,
That gave the limbs large play, and wrapt the form
In easy folds, yet bright with glowing hues
As suited holidays. All hastened on

To that glad bridal. There already stood
The priest prepared to say the spousal rite,
And there the harpers in due order sat,
And there the singers. Sella, midst them all,
Moved strangely and serenely beautiful,
With clear blue eyes, fair locks, and brow and cheek
Colorless as the lily of the lakes,
Yet moulded to such shape as artists give
To beings of immortal youth. Her hands
Had decked her sister for the bridal hour
With chosen flowers, and lawn whose delicate threads
Vied with the spider's spinning. There she stood
With such a gentle pleasure in her looks
As might beseem a river-nymph's soft eyes
Gracing a bridal of the race whose flocks
Were pastured on the borders of her stream.
  She smiled, but from that calm sweet face the smile
Was soon to pass away. That very morn
The elder of the brothers, as he stood
Upon the hillside, had beheld the maid,
Emerging from the channel of the brook,
With three fresh water lilies in her hand,
Wring dry her dripping locks, and in a cleft
Of hanging rock, beside a screen of boughs,
Bestow the spangled slippers. None before
Had known where Sella hid them. Then she laid
The light brown tresses smooth, and in them twined
The lily buds, and hastily drew forth
And threw across her shoulders a light robe

322. The gentle turning-point of the poem. For a moment the Sella of her dreams stands before us; the idealizing of the human creature has been carried to its finest limit, and is arrested now just short of the disappearance of the human soul.

Wrought for the bridal, and with bounding steps
Ran toward the lodge. The youth beheld and marked
The spot and slowly followed from afar.
  Now had the marriage rite been said ; the bride
Stood in the blush that from her burning cheek
Glowed down the alabaster neck, as morn
Crimsons the pearly heaven halfway to the west.
At once the harpers struck their chords ; a gush
Of music broke upon the air ; the youths
All started to the dance. Among them moved
The queenly Sella with a grace that seemed
Caught from the swaying of the summer sea.
The young drew forth the elders to the dance,
Who joined it half abashed, but when they felt
The joyous music tingling in their veins,
They called for quaint old measures, which they trod
As gayly as in youth, and far abroad
Came through the open windows cheerful shouts
And bursts of laughter. They who heard the sound
Upon the mountain footpaths paused and said,
" A merry wedding." Lovers stole away
That sunny afternoon to bowers that edged
The garden walks, and what was whispered there
The lovers of these later times can guess.
  Meanwhile the brothers, when the merry din
Was loudest, stole to where the slippers lay,
And took them thence, and followed down the brook
To where a little rapid rushed between
Its borders of smooth rock, and dropped them in.
The rivulet, as they touched its face, flung up
Its small bright waves like hands, and seemed to take
The prize with eagerness and draw it down.
They, gleaming through the waters as they went,
And striking with light sound the shining stones,

Slid down the stream. The brothers looked and watched
And listened with full beating hearts, till now
The sight and sound had passed, and silently
And half repentant hastened to the lodge.
The sun was near his set; the music rang
Within the dwelling still, but the mirth waned;
For groups of guests were sauntering toward their homes
Across the fields, and far, on hillside paths,
Gleamed the white robes of maidens. Sella grew
Weary of the long merriment; she thought
Of her still haunts beneath the soundless sea,
And all unseen withdrew and sought the cleft
Where she had laid the slippers. They were gone.
She searched the brookside near, yet found them not.
Then her heart sank within her, and she ran
Wildly from place to place, and once again
She searched the secret cleft, and next she stooped
And with spread palms felt carefully beneath
The tufted herbs and bushes, and again,
And yet again she searched the rocky cleft.
"Who could have taken them?" That question cleared
The mystery. She remembered suddenly
That when the dance was in its gayest whirl,
Her brothers were not seen, and when, at length,
They reappeared, the elder joined the sports
With shouts of boisterous mirth, and from her eye
The younger shrank in silence. "Now, I know
The guilty ones," she said, and left the spot,
And stood before the youths with such a look
Of anguish and reproach that well they knew
Her thought, and almost wished the deed undone.

Frankly they owned the charge: "And pardon us;
We did it all in love; we could not bear
That the cold world of waters and the strange
Beings that dwell within it should beguile
Our sister from us." Then they told her all;
How they had seen her stealthily bestow
The slippers in the cleft, and how by stealth
They took them thence and bore them down the brook,
And dropped them in, and how the eager waves
Gathered and drew them down: but at that word
The maiden shrieked — a broken-hearted shriek —
And all who heard it shuddered and turned pale
At the despairing cry, and "They are gone,"
She said, "gone — gone forever. Cruel ones!
'T is you who shut me out eternally
From that serener world which I had learned
To love so well. Why took ye not my life?
Ye cannot know what ye have done." She spake,
And hurried to her chamber, and the guests
Who yet had lingered silently withdrew.
The brothers followed to the maiden's bower,
But with a calm demeanor, as they came,
She met them at the door. "The wrong is great,"
She said, "that ye have done me, but no power
Have ye to make it less, nor yet to soothe
My sorrow; I shall bear it as I may,
The better for the hours that I have passed
In the calm region of the middle sea.
Go, then. I need you not." They, overawed,
Withdrew from that grave presence. Then her tears
Broke forth a flood, as when the August cloud,
Darkening beside the mountain, suddenly
Melts into streams of rain. That weary night
She paced her chamber, murmuring as she walked,

"O peaceful region of the middle sea!
O azure bowers and grots, in which I loved
To roam and rest! Am I to long for you,
And think how strangely beautiful ye are,
Yet never see you more? And dearer yet,
Ye gentle ones in whose sweet company
I trod the shelly pavements of the deep,
And swam its currents, creatures with calm eyes
Looking the tenderest love, and voices soft
As ripple of light waves along the shore,
Uttering the tenderest words! Oh! ne'er again
Shall I, in your mild aspects, read the peace
That dwells within, and vainly shall I pine
To hear your sweet low voices. Haply now
Ye miss me in your deep-sea home, and think
Of me with pity, as of one condemned
To haunt this upper world, with its harsh sounds
And glaring lights, its withering heats, its frosts,
Cruel and killing, its delirious strifes,
And all its feverish passions, till I die."

So mourned she the long night, and when the morn
Brightened the mountains, from her lattice looked
The maiden on a world that was to her
A desolate and dreary waste. That day
She passed in wandering by the brook that oft
Had been her pathway to the sea, and still
Seemed, with its cheerful murmur, to invite
Her footsteps thither. "Well may'st thou rejoice,
Fortunate stream!" she said, "and dance along
Thy bed, and make thy course one ceaseless strain
Of music, for thou journeyest toward the deep,
To which I shall return no more." The night
Brought her to her lone chamber, and she knelt
And prayed, with many tears, to Him whose hand

Touches the wounded heart and it is healed.
With prayer there came new thoughts and new desires.
She asked for patience and a deeper love
For those with whom her lot was henceforth cast,
And that in acts of mercy she might lose
The sense of her own sorrow. When she rose
A weight was lifted from her heart. She sought
Her couch, and slept a long and peaceful sleep.
At morn she woke to a new life. Her days
Henceforth were given to quiet tasks of good
In the great world. Men hearkened to her words,
And wondered at their wisdom and obeyed,
And saw how beautiful the law of love
Can make the cares and toils of daily life.
  Still did she love to haunt the springs and brooks,
As in her cheerful childhood, and she taught
The skill to pierce the soil and meet the veins
Of clear cold water winding underneath,
And call them forth to daylight. From afar
She bade men bring the rivers on long rows
Of pillared arches to the sultry town,
And on the hot air of the summer fling
The spray of dashing fountains. To relieve
Their weary hands, she showed them how to tame
The rushing stream, and make him drive the wheel
That whirls the humming millstone and that wields
The ponderous sledge. The waters of the cloud,
That drench the hillside in the time of rains,
Were gathered at her bidding into pools,

479. In the new life to which Sella awakes, one notes that it is the old world in which she had lived endowed now with those gifts which her ripened soul brought from the ideal world in which she had hoped to lose herself.

And in the months of drought led forth again,
In glimmering rivulets, to refresh the vales,
Till the sky darkened with returning showers.
So passed her life, a long and blameless life,
And far and near her name was named with love
And reverence. Still she kept, as age came on,
Her stately presence; still her eyes looked forth
From under their calm brows as brightly clear
As the transparent wells by which she sat
So oft in childhood. Still she kept her fair
Unwrinkled features, though her locks were white.
A hundred times had summer, since her birth,
Opened the water lily on the lakes,
So old traditions tell, before she died.
A hundred cities mourned her, and her death
Saddened the pastoral valleys. By the brook,
That bickering ran beside the cottage door
Where she was born, they reared her monument.
Ere long the current parted and flowed round
The marble base, forming a little isle,
And there the flowers that love the running stream,
Iris and orchis, and the cardinal flower,
Crowded and hung caressingly around
The stone engraved with Sella's honored name.

THE LITTLE PEOPLE OF THE SNOW.

[In this tender fancy Bryant has treated the personality of the snow with a kinder, more sympathetic touch than poets have been wont to give it. With many the cruelty of cold or its treacherous nature is most significant. Hans Christian Andersen, for example, in the story of *The Ice Maiden* has taken a similar theme, but has emphasized the seductive treachery of the Spirit of Cold. Here Bryant has given the true fairy, innocent of evil purpose, yet inflicting grievous wrong through its nature; sorrowing over the dead Eva, but without the remorse of human beings. The time of the story is placed in legendary antiquity by the exclusion of historic times in lines 35–41, and the antiquity is still more positively affirmed by the lines at the close accounting for our not now seeing the Little People of the Snow. The children had asked for a fairy tale, and it is made more real by being placed at so ethereal a distance.]

Alice. One of your old world stories, Uncle John,
Such as you tell us by the winter fire,
Till we all wonder it has grown so late.
Uncle John. The story of the witch that ground to death
Two children in her mill, or will you have
The tale of Goody Cutpurse?
Alice. Nay now, nay;
Those stories are too childish, Uncle John,
Too childish even for little Willy here,
And I am older, two good years, than he;
No, let us have a tale of elves that ride
By night with jingling reins, or gnomes of the mine,
Or water-fairies, such as you know how
To spin, till Willy's eyes forget to wink,
And good Aunt Mary, busy as she is,
Lays down her knitting.
Uncle John. Listen to me, then.
'T was in the olden time, long, long ago,
And long before the great oak at our door

6. Goody Cut-purse, or Moll Cut-purse, was a famous highway woman of Shakspere's time who robbed people as audaciously as did Jack Sheppard.

Was yet an acorn, on a mountain's side
Lived, with his wife, a cottager. They dwelt
Beside a glen and near a dashing brook,
A pleasant spot in spring, where first the wren
Was heard to chatter, and, among the grass,
Flowers opened earliest; but, when winter came,
That little brook was fringed with other flowers, —
White flowers, with crystal leaf and stem, that grew
In clear November nights. And, later still,
That mountain glen was filled with drifted snows
From side to side, that one might walk across,
While, many a fathom deep, below, the brook
Sang to itself, and leapt and trotted on
Unfrozen, o'er its pebbles, toward the vale.
Alice. A mountain's side, you said; the Alps, perhaps,
Or our own Alleghanies.
Uncle John. Not so fast,
My young geographer, for then the Alps,
With their broad pastures, haply were untrod
Of herdsman's foot, and never human voice
Had sounded in the woods that overhang
Our Alleghany's streams. I think it was
Upon the slopes of the great Caucasus,
Or where the rivulets of Ararat
Seek the Armenian vales. That mountain rose
So high, that, on its top, the winter snow
Was never melted, and the cottagers
Among the summer blossoms, far below,
Saw its white peaks in August from their door.
One little maiden, in that cottage home,
Dwelt with her parents, light of heart and limb,
Bright, restless, thoughtless, flitting here and there
Like sunshine on the uneasy ocean waves,

And sometimes she forgot what she was bid,
As Alice does.
Alice. Or Willy, quite as oft.
Uncle John. But you are older, Alice, two good years,
And should be wiser. Eva was the name
Of this young maiden, now twelve summers old.
Now you must know that, in those early times,
When autumn days grew pale, there came a troop
Of childlike forms from that cold mountain top;
With trailing garments through the air they came,
Or walked the ground with girded loins, and threw
Spangles of silvery frost upon the grass,
And edged the brook with glistening parapets,
And built it crystal bridges, touched the pool,
And turned its face to glass, or, rising thence,
They shook, from their full laps, the soft, light snow,
And buried the great earth, as autumn winds
Bury the forest floor in heaps of leaves.
A beautiful race were they, with baby brows,
And fair, bright locks, and voices like the sound
Of steps on the crisp snow, in which they talked
With man, as friend with friend. A merry sight
It was, when, crowding round the traveller,
They smote him with their heaviest snow-flakes, flung
Needles of frost in handfuls at his cheeks,
And, of the light wreaths of his smoking breath,
Wove a white fringe for his brown beard, and laughed
Their slender laugh to see him wink and grin
And make grim faces as he floundered on.
But, when the spring came on, what terror reigned
Among these Little People of the Snow!
To them the sun's warm beams were shafts of fire,

And the soft south-wind was the wind of death.
Away they flew, all with a pretty scowl
Upon their childish faces, to the north,
Or scampered upward to the mountain's top,
And there defied their enemy, the Spring;
Skipping and dancing on the frozen peaks,
And moulding little snow-balls in their palms,
And rolling them, to crush her flowers below,
Down the steep snow-fields.
Alice. That, too, must have been
A merry sight to look at.
Uncle John. You are right,
But I must speak of graver matters now.
Mid-winter was the time, and Eva stood
Within the cottage, all prepared to dare
The outer cold, with ample furry robe
Close belted round her waist, and boots of fur,
And a broad kerchief, which her mother's hand
Had closely drawn about her ruddy cheek.
"Now, stay not long abroad," said the good dame,
"For sharp is the outer air, and, mark me well,
Go not upon the snow beyond the spot
Where the great linden bounds the neighboring field."
The little maiden promised, and went forth,
And climbed the rounded snow-swells firm with frost
Beneath her feet, and slid, with balancing arms,
Into the hollows. Once, as up a drift
She slowly rose, before her, in the way,
She saw a little creature lily-cheeked,
With flowing flaxen locks, and faint blue eyes,
That gleamed like ice, and robe that only seemed
Of a more shadowy whiteness than her cheek.
On a smooth bank she sat.

Alice. She must have been
One of your Little People of the Snow.
Uncle John. She was so, and, as Eva now drew near,
The tiny creature bounded from her seat;
"And come," she said, "my pretty friend; to-day
We will be playmates. I have watched thee long,
And seen how well thou lov'st to walk these drifts,
And scoop their fair sides into little cells,
And carve them with quaint figures, huge-limbed men,
Lions, and griffins. We will have, to-day,
A merry ramble over these bright fields,
And thou shalt see what thou hast never seen."
On went the pair, until they reached the bound
Where the great linden stood, set deep in snow,
Up to the lower branches. "Here we stop,"
Said Eva, "for my mother has my word
That I will go no farther than this tree."
Then the snow-maiden laughed; "And what is this?
This fear of the pure snow, the innocent snow,
That never harmed aught living? Thou may'st roam
For leagues beyond this garden, and return
In safety; here the grim wolf never prowls,
And here the eagle of our mountain crags
Preys not in winter. I will show the way
And bring thee safely home. Thy mother, sure,
Counselled thee thus because thou hadst no guide."
By such smooth words was Eva won to break

137. The idea of sin is very lightly touched in the poem, and there is no conscious temptation to evil on the part of the Snow-maiden. The absence of a moral sense in the Little People of the Snow is very delicately assumed here. It is with fairies that the poet is dealing, and not with diminutive human beings.

Her promise, and went on with her new friend,
Over the glistening snow and down a bank
Where a white shelf, wrought by the eddying
wind,
Like to a billow's crest in the great sea,
Curtained an opening. "Look, we enter here."
And straight, beneath the fair o'erhanging fold,
Entered the little pair that hill of snow,
Walking along a passage with white walls,
And a white vault above where snow-stars shed
A wintry twilight. Eva moved in awe,
And held her peace, but the snow-maiden smiled,
And talked and tripped along, as, down the way,
Deeper they went into that mountainous drift.
And now the white walls widened, and the vault
Swelled upward, like some vast cathedral dome,
Such as the Florentine, who bore the name
Of Heaven's most potent angel, reared, long since,
Or the unknown builder of that wondrous fane,
The glory of Burgos. Here a garden lay,
In which the Little People of the Snow
Were wont to take their pastime when their tasks
Upon the mountain's side and in the clouds
Were ended. Here they taught the silent frost
To mock, in stem and spray, and leaf and flower,
The growths of summer. Here the palm upreared
Its white columnar trunk and spotless sheaf
Of plume-like leaves; here cedars, huge as those

146. The star form of the snow-crystal gives a peculiar truthfulness to the poet's fancy.

154. *Michael* Angelo, the great Florentine architect, sculptor, and painter.

156. In Bryant's *Letters of a Traveller*, second series, will be found an account of Burgos Cathedral.

Of Lebanon, stretched far their level boughs,
Yet pale and shadowless; the sturdy oak
Stood, with its huge gnarled roots of seeming strength,
Fast anchored in the glistening bank; light sprays
Of myrtle, roses in their bud and bloom,
Drooped by the winding walks; yet all seemed wrought
Of stainless alabaster; up the trees
Ran the lithe jessamine, with stalk and leaf
Colorless as her flowers. "Go softly on,"
Said the snow-maiden; "touch not, with thy hand,
The frail creation round thee, and beware
To sweep it with thy skirts. Now look above.
How sumptuously these bowers are lighted up
With shifting gleams that softly come and go!
These are the northern lights, such as thou seest
In the midwinter nights, cold, wandering flames,
That float, with our processions, through the air;
And, here within our winter palaces,
Mimic the glorious daybreak." Then she told
How, when the wind, in the long winter nights,
Swept the light snows into the hollow dell,
She and her comrades guided to its place
Each wandering flake, and piled them quaintly up,
In shapely colonnade and glistening arch,
With shadowy aisles between, or bade them grow
Beneath their little hands, to bowery walks
In gardens such as these, and, o'er them all,
Built the broad roof. "But thou hast yet to see
A fairer sight," she said, and led the way
To where a window of pellucid ice
Stood in the wall of snow, beside their path.
"Look, but thou may'st not enter." Eva looked,
And lo! a glorious hall, from whose high vault

Stripes of soft light, ruddy, and delicate green,
And tender blue, flowed downward to the floor
And far around, as if the aerial hosts,
That march on high by night, with beamy spears,
And streaming banners, to that place had brought
Their radiant flags to grace a festival.
  And in that hall a joyous multitude
Of those by whom its glistening walls were reared,
Whirled in a merry dance to silvery sounds,
That rang from cymbals of transparent ice,
And ice-cups, quivering to the skilful touch
Of little fingers. Round and round they flew,
As when, in spring, about a chimney top,
A cloud of twittering swallows, just returned,
Wheel round and round, and turn and wheel again,
Unwinding their swift track. So rapidly
Flowed the meandering stream of that fair dance,
Beneath that dome of light. Bright eyes that looked
From under lily brows, and gauzy scarfs
Sparkling like snow-wreaths in the early sun,
Shot by the window in their mazy whirl.
And there stood Eva, wondering at the sight
Of those bright revellers and that graceful sweep
Of motion as they passed her; — long she gazed,
And listened long to the sweet sounds that thrilled
The frosty air, till now the encroaching cold
Recalled her to herself. "Too long, too long
I linger here," she said, and then she sprang
Into the path, and with a hurried step
Followed it upward. Ever by her side
Her little guide kept pace. As on they went
Eva bemoaned her fault: "What must they think —
The dear ones in the cottage, while so long,

Hour after hour, I stay without? I know
That they will seek me far and near, and weep
To find me not. How could I, wickedly,
Neglect the charge they gave me?" As she spoke,
The hot tears started to her eyes; she knelt
In the mid path. "Father! forgive this sin;
Forgive myself I cannot" — thus she prayed,
And rose and hastened onward. When, at last,
They reached the outer air, the clear north breathed
A bitter cold, from which she shrank with dread,
But the snow-maiden bounded as she felt
The cutting blast, and uttered shouts of joy,
And skipped, with boundless glee, from drift to drift,
And danced round Eva, as she labored up
The mounds of snow. "Ah me! I feel my eyes
Grow heavy," Eva said; "they swim with sleep;
I cannot walk for utter weariness,
And I must rest a moment on this bank,
But let it not be long." As thus she spoke,
In half-formed words, she sank on the smooth snow,
With closing lids. Her guide composed the robe
About her limbs, and said, "A pleasant spot
Is this to slumber in; on such a couch
Oft have I slept away the winter night,
And had the sweetest dreams." So Eva slept,
But slept in death; for when the power of frost
Locks up the motions of the living frame,
The victim passes to the realm of Death
Through the dim porch of Sleep. The little guide,
Watching beside her, saw the hues of life
Fade from the fair smooth brow and rounded cheek,
As fades the crimson from a morning cloud,
Till they were white as marble, and the breath
Had ceased to come and go, yet knew she not

At first that this was death. But when she marked
How deep the paleness was, how motionless
That once lithe form, a fear came over her.
She strove to wake the sleeper, plucked her robe,
And shouted in her ear, but all in vain;
The life had passed away from those young limbs.
Then the snow-maiden raised a wailing cry,
Such as the dweller in some lonely wild,
Sleepless through all the long December night,
Hears when the mournful East begins to blow.
  But suddenly was heard the sound of steps,
Grating on the crisp snow; the cottagers
Were seeking Eva; from afar they saw
The twain, and hurried toward them. As they came,
With gentle chidings ready on their lips,
And marked that deathlike sleep, and heard the tale
Of the snow-maiden, mortal anguish fell
Upon their hearts, and bitter words of grief
And blame were uttered: "Cruel, cruel one,
To tempt our daughter thus, and cruel we,
Who suffered her to wander forth alone
In this fierce cold." They lifted the dear child,
And bore her home and chafed her tender limbs,
And strove, by all the simple arts they knew,
To make the chilled blood move, and win the breath
Back to her bosom; fruitlessly they strove.
The little maid was dead. In blank despair
They stood, and gazed at her who never more
Should look on them. "Why die we not with her?"
They said; "without her, life is bitterness."
  Now came the funeral-day; the simple folk
Of all that pastoral region gathered round,
To share the sorrow of the cottagers.

They carved a way into the mound of snow
To the glen's side, and dug a little grave
In the smooth slope, and, following the bier,
In long procession from the silent door,
Chanted a sad and solemn melody :
"Lay her away to rest within the ground.
Yea, lay her down whose pure and innocent life
Was spotless as these snows ; for she was reared
In love, and passed in love life's pleasant spring,
And all that now our tenderest love can do
Is to give burial to her lifeless limbs."
They paused. A thousand slender voices round,
Like echoes softly flung from rock and hill,
Took up the strain, and all the hollow air
Seemed mourning for the dead ; for, on that day,
The Little People of the Snow had come,
From mountain peak, and cloud, and icy hall,
To Eva's burial. As the murmur died,
The funeral-train renewed the solemn chant.
"Thou, Lord, hast taken her to be with Eve,
Whose gentle name was given her. Even so,
For so Thy wisdom saw that it was best
For her and us. We bring our bleeding hearts,
And ask the touch of healing from Thy hand,
As, with submissive tears, we render back
The lovely and beloved to Him who gave."
They ceased. Again the plaintive murmur rose.
From shadowy skirts of low-hung cloud it came,
And wide white fields, and fir-trees capped with snow,
Shivering to the sad sounds. They sank away
To silence in the dim-seen distant woods.
The little grave was closed ; the funeral-train
Departed ; winter wore away ; the spring
Steeped, with her quickening rains, the violet tufts,

By fond hands planted where the maiden slept.
But, after Eva's burial, never more
The Little People of the Snow were seen
By human eye, nor ever human ear
Heard from their lips articulate speech again;
For a decree went forth to cut them off,
Forever, from communion with mankind.
The winter clouds, along the mountain-side
Rolled downward toward the vale, but no fair form
Leaned from their folds, and, in the icy glens,
And aged woods, under snow-loaded pines,
Where once they made their haunt, was emptiness.
  But ever, when the wintry days drew near,
Around that little grave, in the long night,
Frost-wreaths were laid, and tufts of silvery rime
In shape like blades and blossoms of the field,
As one would scatter flowers upon a bier.

MARCH.

THE stormy March is come at last,
  With wind and cloud and changing skies;
I hear the rushing of the blast,
  That through the snowy valley flies.

Ah, passing few are they who speak,
  Wild stormy month! in praise of thee;
Yet, though thy winds are loud and bleak,
  Thou art a welcome month to me.

For thou to northern lands again
  The glad and glorious sun dost bring,

And thou hast joined the gentle train
  And wear'st the gentle name of Spring.

And, in thy reign of blast and storm,
  Smiles many a long, bright, sunny day,
When the changed winds are soft and warm,
  And heaven puts on the blue of May.

Then sing aloud the gushing rills
  In joy that they again are free,
And, brightly leaping down the hills,
  Renew their journey to the sea.

The year's departing beauty hides
  Of wintry storms the sullen threat;
But in thy sternest frown abides
  A look of kindly promise yet.

Thou bring'st the hope of those calm skies,
  And that soft time of sunny showers,
When the wide bloom, on earth that lies,
  Seems of a brighter world than ours.

SONG OF MARION'S MEN.

The exploits of General Francis Marion, the famous partisan warrior of South Carolina, form an intensely interesting chapter in the annals of the American Revolution.

Our band is few but true and tried,
  Our leader frank and bold;
The British soldier trembles
  When Marion's name is told.

Our fortress is the good greenwood,
  Our tent the cypress-tree:
We know the forest round us,
  As seamen know the sea.
We know its walls of thorny vines,
  Its glades of reedy grass,
Its safe and silent islands
  Within the dark morass.

Woe to the English soldiery
  That little dread us near!
On them shall light at midnight
  A strange and sudden fear:
When, waking to their tents on fire,
  They grasp their arms in vain,
And they who stand to face us
  Are beat to earth again;
And they who fly in terror deem
  A mighty host behind,
And hear the tramp of thousands
  Upon the hollow wind.

Then sweet the hour that brings release
  From danger and from toil:
We talk the battle over,
  And share the battle's spoil.
The woodland rings with laugh and shout,
  As if a hunt were up,
And woodland flowers are gathered
  To crown the soldier's cup.
With merry songs we mock the wind
  That in the pine-top grieves,
And slumber long and sweetly
  On beds of oaken leaves.

Well knows the fair and friendly moon
The band that Marion leads —
The glitter of their rifles,
The scampering of their steeds.
'T is life to guide the fiery barb
Across the moonlight plain;
'T is life to feel the night-wind
That lifts the tossing mane.
A moment in the British camp —
A moment — and away
Back to the pathless forest
Before the peep of day.

Grave men there are by broad Santee,
Grave men with hoary hairs;
Their hearts are all with Marion,
For Marion are their prayers.
And lovely ladies greet our band
With kindliest welcoming,
With smiles like those of summer,
And tears like those of spring.
For them we wear these trusty arms,
And lay them down no more
Till we have driven the Briton,
Forever, from our shore.

THE GREEN MOUNTAIN BOYS.

This song refers to the expedition of the Vermonters, commanded by Ethan Allen, by whom the British fort of Ticonderoga, on Lake Champlain, was surprised and taken, in May, 1775. — W. C. B.

HERE halt we our march, and pitch our tent
On the rugged forest-ground,

And light our fire with the branches rent
  By winds from the beeches round.
Wild storms have torn this ancient wood,
  But a wilder is at hand,
With hail of iron and rain of blood
  To sweep and waste the land.

How the dark wood rings with our voices shrill,
  That startle the sleeping bird!
To-morrow eve must the voice be still,
  And the step must fall unheard.
The Briton lies by the blue Champlain,
  In Ticonderoga's towers,
And ere the sun rise twice again,
  Must they and the lake be ours.

Fill up the bowl from the brook that glides
  Where the fire-flies light the brake;
A ruddier juice the Briton hides
  In his fortress by the lake.
Build high the fire, till the panther leap
  From his lofty perch in flight,
And we'll strengthen our weary arms with sleep
  For the deeds of to-morrow night.

THE GREEK PARTISAN.

The Greek war for independence from Turkish rule was opened by the inspiration of Alexander Ypsilanti in 1820 and closed with the Peace of Adrianople in 1826. Those who have read Whittier's *Snow-Bound* will recall the reference there to the great Greek partisan with his

"Mainote Greeks,
A Turk's head at each saddle-bow!"

Our free flag is dancing
  In the free mountain air,
And burnished arms are glancing,
  And warriors gathering there;
And fearless is the little train
  Whose gallant bosoms shield it;
The blood that warms their hearts shall stain
  That banner, ere they yield it.
Each dark eye is fixed on earth,
  And brief each solemn greeting;
There is no look nor sound of mirth,
  Where those stern men are meeting.

They go to the slaughter
  To strike the sudden blow,
And pour on earth, like water,
  The best blood of the foe;
To rush on them from rock and height,
  And clear the narrow valley,
Or fire their camp at dead of night,
  And fly before they rally.
Chains are round our country pressed,
  And cowards have betrayed her,
And we must make her bleeding breast
  The grave of the invader.

Not till from her fetters
  We raise up Greece again,
And write, in bloody letters,
  That tyranny is slain, —
Oh, not till then the smile shall steal
  Across those darkened faces,
Nor one of all those warriors feel
  His children's dear embraces.

Reap we not the ripened wheat,
Till yonder hosts are flying,
And all their bravest, at our feet,
Like autumn sheaves are lying.

THE CONQUEROR'S GRAVE.

Within this lowly grave a Conqueror lies,
And yet the monument proclaims it not,
Nor round the sleeper's name hath chisel wrought
The emblems of a fame that never dies, —
Ivy and amaranth, in a graceful sheaf,
Twined with the laurel's fair, imperial leaf.
A simple name alone,
To the great world unknown,
Is graven here, and wild-flowers, rising round,
Meek meadow-sweet and violets of the ground,
Lean lovingly against the humble stone.

Here, in the quiet earth, they laid apart
No man of iron mould and bloody hands,
Who sought to wreak upon the cowering lands
The passions that consumed his restless heart;
But one of tender spirit and delicate frame,
Gentlest, in mien and mind,
Of gentle womankind,
Timidly shrinking from the breath of blame:
One in whose eyes the smile of kindness made
Its haunt, like flowers by sunny brooks in May,
Yet, at the thought of others' pain, a shade
Of sweeter sadness chased the smile away.

Nor deem that when the hand that moulders here
Was raised in menace, realms were chilled with fear,

And armies mustered at the sign, as when
Clouds rise on clouds before the rainy East—
Gray captains leading bands of veteran men
And fiery youths to be the vulture's feast.
Not thus were waged the mighty wars that gave
The victory to her who fills this grave:
Alone her task was wrought,
Alone the battle fought;
Through that long strife her constant hope was staid
On God alone, nor looked for other aid.

She met the hosts of Sorrow with a look
That altered not beneath the frown they wore,
And soon the lowering brood were tamed, and took,
Meekly, her gentle rule, and frowned no more.
Her soft hand put aside the assaults of wrath,
And calmly broke in twain
The fiery shafts of pain,
And rent the nets of passion from her path.
By that victorious hand despair was slain.
With love she vanquished hate and overcame
Evil with good, in her Great Master's name.

Her glory is not of this shadowy state,
Glory that with the fleeting season dies;
But when she entered at the sapphire gate
What joy was radiant in celestial eyes!
How heaven's bright depths with sounding welcomes rung,
And flowers of heaven by shining hands were flung!
And He who, long before,
Pain, scorn, and sorrow bore,
The Mighty Sufferer, with aspect sweet,
Smiled on the timid stranger from his seat;

He who returning, glorious, from the grave,
Dragged Death, disarmed, in chains, a crouching
slave.

See, as I linger here, the sun grows low;
Cool airs are murmuring that the night is near.
Oh, gentle sleeper, from thy grave I go
Consoled though sad, in hope and yet in fear.
Brief is the time, I know,
The warfare scarce begun;
Yet all may win the triumphs thou hast won.
Still flows the fount whose waters strengthened thee,
The victors' names are yet too few to fill
Heaven's mighty roll; the glorious armory,
That ministered to thee, is opened still.

THE HUNTER OF THE PRAIRIES.

Ay, this is freedom! — these pure skies
Were never stained with village smoke:
The fragrant wind, that through them flies,
Is breathed from wastes by plough unbroke.
Here, with my rifle and my steed,
And her who left the world for me,
I plant me, where the red deer feed
In the green desert — and am free.

For here the fair savannas know
No barriers in the bloomy grass;
Wherever breeze of heaven may blow,
Or beam of heaven may glance, I pass.
In pastures, measureless as air,

The bison is my noble game;
The bounding elk, whose antlers tear
The branches, falls before my aim.

Mine are the river-fowl that scream
From the long stripe of waving sedge;
The bear that marks my weapon's gleam,
Hides vainly in the forest's edge;
In vain the she-wolf stands at bay;
The brinded catamount, that lies
High in the boughs to watch his prey,
Even in the act of springing, dies.

With what free growth the elm and plane
Fling their huge arms across my way,
Gray, old, and cumbered with a train
Of vines, as huge, and old, and gray!
Free stray the lucid streams, and find
No taint in these fresh lawns and shades;
Free spring the flowers that scent the wind
Where never scythe has swept the glades.

Alone the Fire, when frost-winds sere
The heavy herbage of the ground,
Gathers his annual harvest here,
With roaring like the battle's sound,
And hurrying flames that sweep the plain,
And smoke-streams gushing up the sky:
I meet the flames with flames again,
And at my door they cower and die.

Here, from dim woods, the aged past
Speaks solemnly; and I behold
The boundless future in the vast

And lonely river, seaward rolled.
Who feeds its founts with rain and dew?
Who moves, I ask, its gliding mass,
And trains the bordering vines, whose blue,
Bright clusters tempt me as I pass?

Broad are these streams — my steed obeys,
Plunges, and bears me through the tide.
Wide are these woods — I thread the maze
Of giant stems, nor ask a guide.
I hunt till day's last glimmer dies
O'er woody vale and grassy height;
And kind the voice and glad the eyes
That welcome my return at night.

THE YELLOW VIOLET.

When beechen buds begin to swell,
And woods the bluebird's warble know,
The yellow violet's modest bell
Peeps from the last year's leaves below.

Ere russet fields their green resume,
Sweet flower, I love, in forest bare,
To meet thee, when thy faint perfume
Alone is in the virgin air.

Of all her train, the hands of Spring
First plant thee in the watery mould,
And I have seen thee blossoming
Beside the snow-bank's edges cold.

Thy parent sun, who bade thee view
  Pale skies, and chilling moisture sip,
Has bathed thee in his own bright hue,
  And streaked with jet thy glowing lip.

Yet slight thy form, and low thy seat,
  And earthward bent thy gentle eye,
Unapt the passing view to meet,
  When loftier flowers are flaunting nigh.

Oft, in the sunless April day,
  Thy early smile has stayed my walk;
But midst the gorgeous blooms of May,
  I passed thee on thy humble stalk.

So they, who climb to wealth, forget
  The friends in darker fortunes tried.
I copied them — but I regret
  That I should ape the ways of pride.

And when again the genial hour
  Awakes the painted tribes of light,
I'll not o'erlook the modest flower
  That made the woods of April bright.

TO THE FRINGED GENTIAN.

Thou blossom bright with autumn dew,
And colored with the heaven's own blue,
That openest when the quiet light
Succeeds the keen and frosty night.

Thou comest not when violets lean
O'er wandering brooks and springs unseen.

Or columbines, in purple dressed,
Nod o'er the ground-bird's hidden nest.

Thou waitest late and com'st alone,
When woods are bare and birds are flown,
And frosts and shortening days portend
The aged year is near his end.

Then doth thy sweet and quiet eye
Look through its fringes to the sky,
Blue — blue — as if that sky let fall
A flower from its cerulean wall.

I would that thus, when I shall see
The hour of death draw near to me,
Hope, blossoming within my heart,
May look to heaven as I depart.

THE DEATH OF THE FLOWERS.

The melancholy days are come, the saddest of the year,
Of wailing winds, and naked woods, and meadows brown and sere.
Heaped in the hollows of the grove, the autumn leaves lie dead;
They rustle to the eddying gust, and to the rabbit's tread;
The robin and the wren are flown, and from the shrubs the jay,
And from the wood-top calls the crow through all the gloomy day.

Where are the flowers, the fair young flowers, that lately sprang and stood
In brighter light and softer airs, a beauteous sisterhood?
Alas! they all are in their graves, the gentle race of flowers
Are lying in their lowly beds, with the fair and good of ours.
The rain is falling where they lie, but the cold November rain
Calls not from out the gloomy earth the lovely ones again.

The wind-flower and the violet, they perished long ago,
And the brier-rose and the orchis died amid the summer glow;
But on the hills the golden-rod, and the aster in the wood,
And the yellow sun-flower by the brook in autumn beauty stood,
Till fell the frost from the clear cold heaven, as falls the plague on men,
And the brightness of their smile was gone, from upland, glade, and glen.

And now, when comes the calm mild day, as still such days will come,
To call the squirrel and the bee from out their winter home;
When the sound of dropping nuts is heard, though all the trees are still,
And twinkle in the smoky light the waters of the rill,
The south wind searches for the flowers whose fragrance late he bore,
And sighs to find them in the wood and by the stream no more.

And then I think of one who in her youthful beauty died,
The fair meek blossom that grew up and faded by my side.
In the cold moist earth we laid her, when the forests cast the leaf,
And we wept that one so lovely should have a life so brief:
Yet not unmeet it was that one, like that young friend of ours,
So gentle and so beautiful, should perish with the flowers.

"INNOCENT CHILD AND SNOW-WHITE FLOWER."

INNOCENT child and snow-white flower!
Well are ye paired in your opening hour.
Thus should the pure and the lovely meet,
Stainless with stainless, and sweet with sweet.

White as those leaves, just blown apart,
Are the folds of thy own young heart;
Guilty passion and cankering care
Never have left their traces there.

Artless one! though thou gazest now
O'er the white blossom with earnest brow,
Soon will it tire thy childish eye;
Fair as it is, thou wilt throw it by.

25. This last verse, as indeed the whole poem, is called out by the poet's sorrow over the remembered death of his sister, a few years before.

Throw it aside in thy weary hour,
Throw to the ground the fair white flower;
Yet, as thy tender years depart,
Keep that white and innocent heart.

ROBERT OF LINCOLN.

Merrily swinging on brier and weed,
  Near to the nest of his little dame,
Over the mountain-side or mead,
  Robert of Lincoln is telling his name:
      Bob-o'-link, bob-o'-link,
      Spink, spank, spink;
Snug and safe is that nest of ours,
Hidden among the summer flowers.
      Chee, chee, chee.

Robert of Lincoln is gayly drest,
  Wearing a bright black wedding-coat;
White are his shoulders and white his crest.
  Hear him call in his merry note:
      Bob-o'-link, bob-o'-link,
      Spink, spank, spink;
Look, what a nice new coat is mine,
Sure there was never a bird so fine.
      Chee, chee, chee.

Robert of Lincoln's Quaker wife,
  Pretty and quiet, with plain brown wings,
Passing at home a patient life,
  Broods in the grass while her husband sings:
      Bob-o'-link, bob-o'-link,
      Spink, spank, spink;

Brood, kind creature; you need not fear
Thieves and robbers while I am here.
Chee, chee, chee.

Modest and shy as a nun is she;
One weak chirp is her only note.
Braggart and prince of braggarts is he,
Pouring boasts from his little throat:
Bob-o'-link, bob-o'-link,
Spink, spank, spink;
Never was I afraid of man;
Catch me, cowardly knaves, if you can!
Chee, chee, chee.

Six white eggs on a bed of hay,
Flecked with purple, a pretty sight!
There as the mother sits all day,
Robert is singing with all his might:
Bob-o'-link, bob-o'-link,
Spink, spank, spink;
Nice good wife, that never goes out,
Keeping house while I frolic about.
Chee, chee, chee.

Soon as the little ones chip the shell,
Six wide mouths are open for food;
Robert of Lincoln bestirs him well,
Gathering seeds for the hungry brood.
Bob-o'-link, bob-o'-link,
Spink, spank, spink;
This new life is likely to be
Hard for a gay young fellow like me.
Chee, chee, chee.

Robert of Lincoln at length is made
Sober with work, and silent with care;
Off is his holiday garment laid,
Half forgotten that merry air:
Bob-o'-link, bob-o'-link,
Spink, spank, spink;
Nobody knows but my mate and I
Where our nest and our nestlings lie.
Chee, chee, chee.

Summer wanes; the children are grown;
Fun and frolic no more he knows;
Robert of Lincoln's a humdrum crone;
Off he flies, and we sing as he goes:
Bob-o'-link, bob-o'-link,
Spink, spank, spink;
When you can pipe that merry old strain,
Robert of Lincoln, come back again.
Chee, chee, chee.

TO A WATERFOWL.

This poem was one of eight, namely: *The Ages, To a Waterfowl, Version of a Fragment from Simonides, Inscription for the Entrance to a Wood, The Yellow Violet, Song, Green River, Thanatopsis*, which formed a little collection of his poems put forth by Bryant in 1821, when he was in his twenty-seventh year. It marks the beginning of the classical period of American poetry. It was eighteen years later that Longfellow's *Voices of the Night* was published. Shelley's poem, *To a Skylark*, was written in 1820.

WHITHER, midst falling dew,
While glow the heavens with the last steps of day,
Far, through their rosy depths, dost thou pursue
Thy solitary way?

Vainly the fowler's eye
Might mark thy distant flight to do thee wrong,
As, darkly seen against the crimson sky,
Thy figure floats along.

8. Bryant had written: —

"As darkly painted on the crimson sky,"

but before publishing had changed the line to its present form. He was at the time in frequent correspondence with Richard Henry Dana, father of the author of *Two Years before the Mast*, and himself a poet, and fastidious critic. Dana wrote: —

"In that delicatest of delicate little poems, the *Waterfowl*, I am told that you have substituted some commonplace word — I forget it now — for 'painted.' Why! it adorns the whole picture, makes complete to the mind (the poetic, susceptible mind, I mean) the crimson background and the darkly floating *bird*, and envelops him in an atmosphere all aglow, and rounds the several objects with a harmonizing whole." To this, Bryant replied in defence of his change:

"I was never satisfied with the word 'painted,' because the next line is: —

"Thy figure *floats* along."

Now, from a very early period — I am not sure that it was not from the very time that I wrote the poem — there seemed to me an incongruity between the idea of a figure painted on the sky and a figure moving, 'floating' across its face. If the figure were painted, then it would be fixed. The incongruity distressed me, and I could not be easy until I had made the change. I preferred a plain prosaic expression to a picturesque one which seemed to me false. 'Painted' expresses well the depth and strength of color which fixed my attention when I saw the bird, — for the scene was founded on a real incident, — but it contradicted the motion of the winds and the progress of the bird through the air. So you have my defence."

Seek'st thou the plashy brink
Of weedy lake, or marge of river wide,
Or where the rocking billows rise and sink
On the chafed ocean-side?

There is a Power whose care
Teaches thy way along that pathless coast —
The desert and illimitable air —
Lone wandering, but not lost.

All day thy wings have fanned,
At that far height, the cold, thin atmosphere,
Yet stoop not, weary, to the welcome land,
Though the dark night is near.

And soon that toil shall end;
Soon shalt thou find a summer home, and rest,
And scream among thy fellows; reeds shall bend,
Soon, o'er thy sheltered nest.

Thou 'rt gone, the abyss of heaven
Hath swallowed up thy form; yet, on my heart
Deeply has sunk the lesson thou hast given,
And shall not soon depart.

He who, from zone to zone,
Guides through the boundless sky thy certain flight,
In the long way that I must tread alone,
Will lead my steps aright.

THE WHITE-FOOTED DEER.

"During the stay of Long's Expedition at Engineer Cantonment, three specimens of a variety of the common deer were brought in, having all the feet white near the hoofs, and extending to those on the hind-feet from a little above the spurious hoofs. This white extremity was divided, upon the sides of the foot, by the general color of the leg, which extends down near to the hoofs, leaving a white triangle in front, of which the point was elevated rather higher than the spurious hoofs." — GODMAN'S *Natural History*, vol. ii., p. 314. W. C. B.

It was a hundred years ago,
  When, by the woodland ways,
The traveller saw the wild-deer drink,
  Or crop the birchen sprays.

Beneath a hill, whose rocky side
  O'erbrowed a grassy mead,
And fenced a cottage from the wind,
  A deer was wont to feed.

She only came when on the cliffs
  The evening moonlight lay,
And no man knew the secret haunts
  In which she walked by day.

White were her feet, her forehead showed
  A spot of silvery white,
That seemed to glimmer like a star
  In autumn's hazy night.

And here, when sang the whippoorwill,
  She cropped the sprouting leaves,

And here her rustling steps were heard
  On still October eves.

But when the broad midsummer moon
  Rose o'er that grassy lawn,
Beside the silver-footed deer
  There grazed a spotted fawn.

The cottage dame forbade her son
  To aim the rifle here;
"It were a sin," she said, "to harm
  Or fright that friendly deer.

"This spot has been my pleasant home
  Ten peaceful years and more;
And ever, when the moonlight shines,
  She feeds before our door.

"The red-men say that here she walked
  A thousand moons ago;
They never raise the war-whoop here,
  And never twang the bow.

"I love to watch her as she feeds,
  And think that all is well
While such a gentle creature haunts
  The place in which we dwell."

The youth obeyed, and sought for game
  In forests far away,
Where, deep in silence and in moss,
  The ancient woodland lay.

But once, in autumn's golden time
  He ranged the wild in vain,

Nor roused the pheasant nor the deer,
And wandered home again.

The crescent moon and crimson eve
Shone with a mingling light;
The deer, upon the grassy mead,
Was feeding full in sight.

He raised the rifle to his eye,
And from the cliffs around
A sudden echo, shrill and sharp,
Gave back its deadly sound.

Away, into the neighboring wood,
The startled creature flew,
And crimson drops at morning lay
Amid the glimmering dew.

Next evening shone the waxing moon
As brightly as before;
The deer upon the grassy mead
Was seen again no more.

But ere that crescent moon was old,
By night the red-men came,
And burnt the cottage to the ground,
And slew the youth and dame.

Now woods have overgrown the mead,
And hid the cliffs from sight;
There shrieks the hovering hawk at noon,
And prowls the fox at night.

THE HUNTER'S SERENADE.

THY bower is finished, fairest!
  Fit bower for hunter's bride,
Where old woods overshadow
  The green savanna's side.
I 've wandered long, and wandered far.
  And never have I met,
In all this lovely Western land,
  A spot so lovely yet.
But I shall think it fairer
  When thou art come to bless,
With thy sweet smile and silver voice,
  Its silent loveliness.

For thee the wild-grape glistens
  On sunny knoll and tree,
The slim papaya ripens
  Its yellow fruit for thee.
For thee the duck, on glassy stream,
  The prairie-fowl shall die;
My rifle for thy feast shall bring
  The wild-swan from the sky.
The forest's leaping panther,
  Fierce, beautiful, and fleet,
Shall yield his spotted hide to be
  A carpet for thy feet.

I know, for thou hast told me,
  Thy maiden love of flowers;
Ah, those that deck thy gardens
  Are pale compared with ours,

15. *Papaya.* The papaw or custard-apple.

When our wide woods and mighty lawns
  Bloom to the April skies,
The earth has no more gorgeous sight
  To show to human eyes.
In meadows red with blossoms,
  All summer long, the bee
Murmurs, and loads his yellow thighs,
  For thee, my love, and me.

Or wouldst thou gaze at tokens
  Of ages long ago —
Our old oaks stream with mosses,
  And sprout with mistletoe;
And mighty vines, like serpents, climb
  The giant sycamore;
And trunks, o'erthrown for centuries,
  Cumber the forest floor;
And in the great savanna,
  The solitary mound,
Built by the elder world, o'erlooks
  The loneliness around.

Come, thou hast not forgotten
  Thy pledge and promise quite,
With many blushes murmured,
  Beneath the evening light.
Come, the young violets crowd my door,
  Thy earliest look to win,
And at my silent window-sill
  The jessamine peeps in.
All day the red-bird warbles
  Upon the mulberry near,
And the night-sparrow trills her song
  All night, with none to hear.

THE PLANTING OF THE APPLE-TREE.

COME, let us plant the apple-tree.
Cleave the tough greensward with the spade;
Wide let its hollow bed be made;
There gently lay the roots, and there
Sift the dark mould with kindly care,
And press it o'er them tenderly,
As, round the sleeping infant's feet,
We softly fold the cradle-sheet;
So plant we the apple-tree.

What plant we in this apple-tree?
Buds, which the breath of summer days
Shall lengthen into leafy sprays;
Boughs where the thrush, with crimson breast,
Shall haunt and sing and hide her nest;
We plant, upon the sunny lea,
A shadow for the noontide hour,
A shelter from the summer shower,
When we plant the apple-tree.

What plant we in this apple-tree?
Sweets for a hundred flowery springs
To load the May-wind's restless wings,
When, from the orchard-row, he pours
Its fragrance through our open doors;
A world of blossoms for the bee,
Flowers for the sick girl's silent room,
For the glad infant sprigs of bloom,
We plant with the apple-tree.

What plant we in this apple-tree?
Fruits that shall swell in sunny June,

And redden in the August noon,
And drop, when gentle airs come by,
That fan the blue September sky,
While children come, with cries of glee,
And seek them where the fragrant grass
Betrays their bed to those who pass,
At the foot of the apple-tree.

And when, above this apple-tree,
The winter stars are quivering bright,
And winds go howling through the night,
Girls, whose young eyes o'erflow with mirth,
Shall peel its fruit by cottage-hearth,
And guests in prouder homes shall see,
Heaped with the grape of Cintra's vine
And golden orange of the line,
The fruit of the apple-tree.

The fruitage of this apple-tree
Winds and our flag of stripe and star
Shall bear to coasts that lie afar,
Where men shall wonder at the view,
And ask in what fair groves they grew;
And sojourners beyond the sea
Shall think of childhood's careless day,
And long, long hours of summer play,
In the shade of the apple-tree.

Each year shall give this apple-tree
A broader flush of roseate bloom,
A deeper maze of verdurous gloom,
And loosen, when the frost-clouds lower,
The crisp brown leaves in thicker shower.
The years shall come and pass, but we

Shall hear no longer, where we lie,
The summer's songs, the autumn's sigh,
  In the boughs of the apple-tree.

  And time shall waste this apple-tree.
Oh, when its aged branches throw
Thin shadows on the ground below,
Shall fraud and force and iron will
Oppress the weak and helpless still?
  What shall the tasks of mercy be,
Amid the toils, the strifes, the tears
Of those who live when length of years
  Is wasting this little apple-tree?

  "Who planted this old apple-tree?"
The children of that distant day
Thus to some aged man shall say;
And, gazing on its mossy stem,
The gray-haired man shall answer them:
  "A poet of the land was he,
Born in the rude but good old times;
'T is said he made some quaint old rhymes,
  On planting the apple-tree."

73. In a letter to Dr. Orville Dewey, written from New York in November, 1846, Bryant writes: "I have been, and am, at my place on Long Island, planting and transplanting trees, in the mist, sixty or seventy; some for shade, most for fruit. Hereafter, men, whose existence is at present merely possible, will gather pears from the trees which I have set in the ground, and wonder what old *covey*, — for in those days the slang terms of the present time, by the ordinary process of change in languages, will have become classical, — what old *covey* of past ages planted them?" The poem was written in 1849, but not published until 1864.

A FOREST HYMN.

The groves were God's first temples. Ere man learned
To hew the shaft, and lay the architrave,
And spread the roof above them — ere he framed
The lofty vault, to gather and roll back
The sound of anthems; in the darkling wood,
Amid the cool and silence, he knelt down,
And offered to the Mightiest solemn thanks
And supplication. For his simple heart
Might not resist the sacred influence
Which, from the stilly twilight of the place,
And from the gray old trunks that high in heaven
Mingled their mossy boughs, and from the sound
Of the invisible breath that swayed at once
All their green tops, stole over him, and bowed
His spirit with the thought of boundless power
And inaccessible majesty. Ah, why
Should we, in the world's riper years, neglect
God's ancient sanctuaries, and adore
Only among the crowd, and under roofs
That our frail hands have raised? Let me, at least,
Here, in the shadow of this aged wood,
Offer one hymn — thrice happy, if it find
Acceptance in His ear.

Father, thy hand
Hath reared these venerable columns, thou
Didst weave this verdant roof. Thou didst look down
Upon the naked earth, and, forthwith, rose
All these fair ranks of trees. They, in thy sun,
Budded, and shook their green leaves in thy breeze,
And shot toward heaven. The century-living crow

Whose birth was in their tops, grew old and died
Among their branches, till, at last, they stood,
As now they stand, massy, and tall, and dark,
Fit shrine for humble worshipper to hold
Communion with his Maker. These dim vaults,
These winding aisles, of human pomp or pride
Report not. No fantastic carvings show
The boast of our vain race to change the form
Of thy fair works. But thou art here — thou fill'st
The solitude. Thou art in the soft winds
That run along the summit of these trees
In music; thou art in the cooler breath
That from the inmost darkness of the place
Comes, scarcely felt; the barky trunks, the ground,
The fresh moist ground, are all instinct with thee.
Here is continual worship; — Nature, here,
In the tranquillity that thou dost love,
Enjoys thy presence. Noiselessly, around,
From perch to perch, the solitary bird
Passes; and yon clear spring, that, midst its herbs,
Wells softly forth and wandering steeps the roots
Of half the mighty forest, tells no tale

34–36. As originally printed, these lines stood as follows: —

"Communion with his Maker. Here are seen
No traces of man's pomp or pride. No silks
Rustle; no jewels shine; nor envious eyes
Encounter. No fantastic carvings show."

"Christopher North" (John Wilson) criticises in *Blackwood's Magazine* (April, 1832), the introduction of silks, jewels, and envious critical eyes as jarring upon the mind. "The grandeur of the grove temple," he says, "and the sincerity of the grove worship, needed not such paltry contrasts to make them impressive." Bryant at once saw the justness of the stricture, and dropped the objectionable lines.

50. This line as first written read: —

"Wells softly forth and visits the stray roots."

Of all the good it does. Thou hast not left
Thyself without a witness, in the shades,
Of thy perfections. Grandeur, strength, and grace
Are here to speak of thee. This mighty oak —
By whose immovable stem I stand and seem
Almost annihilated — not a prince,
In all that proud old world beyond the deep,
E'er wore his crown as loftily as he
Wears the green coronal of leaves with which
Thy hand has graced him. Nestled at his root
Is beauty, such as blooms not in the glare
Of the broad sun. That delicate forest flower,
With scented breath and look so like a smile,
Seems, as it issues from the shapeless mould,
An emanation of the indwelling Life,
A visible token of the upholding Love,
That are the soul of this great universe.

My heart is awed within me when I think
Of the great miracle that still goes on,
In silence, round me — the perpetual work
Of thy creation, finished, yet renewed
Forever. Written on thy works I read
The lesson of thy own eternity.
Lo! all grow old and die — but see again,
How on the faltering footsteps of decay
Youth presses — ever gay and beautiful youth
In all its beautiful forms. These lofty trees
Wave not less proudly that their ancestors
Moulder beneath them. Oh, there is not lost
One of earth's charms: upon her bosom yet,
After the flight of untold centuries,
The freshness of her far beginning lies
And yet shall lie. Life mocks the idle hate

Of his arch-enemy Death — yea, seats himself
Upon the tyrant's throne — the sepulchre,
And of the triumphs of his ghastly foe
Makes his own nourishment. For he came forth
From thine own bosom, and shall have no end.

There have been holy men who hid themselves
Deep in the woody wilderness, and gave
Their lives to thought and prayer, till they outlived
The generation born with them, nor seemed
Less aged than the hoary trees and rocks
Around them; — and there have been holy men
Who deemed it were not well to pass life thus.
But let me often to these solitudes
Retire, and in thy presence reassure
My feeble virtue. Here its enemies,
The passions, at thy plainer footsteps shrink
And tremble and are still. O God! when thou
Dost scare the world with tempests, set on fire
The heavens with falling thunderbolts, or fill,
With all the waters of the firmament,
The swift dark whirlwind that uproots the woods
And drowns the villages; when, at thy call,
Uprises the great deep and throws himself

86. This line originally read: —

"Upon the sepulchre, and blooms and smiles."

Mr. Dana raised objections, and Bryant, replying, wrote: "I remember very well when I wrote the word 'blooms' that I had a vague idea of its impropriety, but I did not know why until you showed me. I have rung half a dozen changes on the faulty line. You shall choose: —

'Upon the tyrant's throne — the sepulchre,'
'As in defiance, on the sepulchre,'
'In loneliness upon the sepulchre.'"

Upon the continent, and overwhelms
Its cities — who forgets not, at the sight
Of these tremendous tokens of thy power,
His pride, and lays his strifes and follies by?
Oh, from these sterner aspects of thy face
Spare me and mine, nor let us need the wrath
Of the mad unchained elements to teach
Who rules them. Be it ours to meditate,
In these calm shades, thy milder majesty,
And to the beautiful order of thy works
Learn to conform the order of our lives.

"O FAIREST OF THE RURAL MAIDS."

O fairest of the rural maids!
Thy birth was in the forest shades;
Green boughs, and glimpses of the sky,
Were all that met thine infant eye.

Thy sports, thy wanderings, when a child,
Were ever in the sylvan wild;
And all the beauty of the place
Is in thy heart and on thy face.

The twilight of the trees and rocks
Is in the light shade of thy locks;
Thy step is as the wind, that weaves
Its playful way among the leaves.

Thine eyes are springs, in whose serene
And silent waters heaven is seen;

1. The only one of the poet's love poems which he chose to preserve in print. It was addressed to Miss Fanny Fairchild, whom he afterward married.

Their lashes are the herbs that look
On their young figures in the brook.

The forest depths, by foot unpressed,
Are not more sinless than thy breast;
The holy peace, that fills the air
Of those calm solitudes, is there.

A SUMMER RAMBLE.

The quiet August noon has come;
  A slumberous silence fills the sky,
The fields are still, the woods are dumb,
  In glassy sleep the waters lie.

And mark yon soft white clouds that rest
  Above our vale, a moveless throng;
The cattle on the mountain's breast
  Enjoy the grateful shadow long.

Oh, how unlike those merry hours,
  In early June, when Earth laughs out,
When the fresh winds make love to flowers,
  And woodlands sing and waters shout.

When in the grass sweet voices talk,
  And strains of tiny music swell
From every moss-cup of the rock,
  From every nameless blossom's bell.

But now a joy too deep for sound,
  A peace no other season knows,
Hushes the heavens and wraps the ground,
  The blessing of supreme repose.

Away! I will not be, to-day,
The only slave of toil and care.
Away from desk and dust! away!
I 'll be as idle as the air.

Beneath the open sky abroad,
Among the plants and breathing things,
The sinless, peaceful works of God,
I 'll share the calm the season brings.

Come, thou, in whose soft eyes I see
The gentle meanings of thy heart,
One day amid the woods with me,
From men and all their cares apart.

And where, upon the meadow's breast,
The shadow of the thicket lies,
The blue wild-flowers thou gatherest
Shall glow yet deeper near thine eyes.

Come, and when mid the calm profound,
I turn, those gentle eyes to seek,
They, like the lovely landscape round,
Of innocence and peace shall speak.

Rest here, beneath the unmoving shade,
And on the silent valleys gaze,
Winding and widening, till they fade
In yon soft ring of summer haze.

The village trees their summits rear
Still as its spire, and yonder flock
At rest in those calm fields appear
As chiselled from the lifeless rock.

One tranquil mount the scene o'erlooks —
There the hushed winds their sabbath keep,
While a near hum from bees and brooks
Comes faintly like the breath of sleep.

Well may the gazer deem that when,
Worn with the struggle and the strife,
And heart-sick at the wrongs of men,
The good forsakes the scene of life;

Like this deep quiet that, awhile,
Lingers the lovely landscape o'er,
Shall be the peace whose holy smile
Welcomes him to a happier shore.

THE LAND OF DREAMS.

A MIGHTY realm is the Land of Dreams,
With steeps that hang in the twilight sky,
And weltering oceans and trailing streams,
That gleam where the dusky valleys lie.

But over its shadowy border flow
Sweet rays from the world of endless morn,
And the nearer mountains catch the glow,
And flowers in the nearer fields are born.

The souls of the happy dead repair,
From their bowers of light, to that bordering land,
And walk in the fainter glory there,
With the souls of the living hand in hand.

One calm sweet smile, in that shadowy sphere,
From eyes that open on earth no more —

One warning word from a voice once dear —
  How they rise in the memory o'er and o'er!

Far off from those hills that shine with day,
  And fields that bloom in the heavenly gales.
The Land of Dreams goes stretching away
  To dimmer mountains and darker vales.

There lie the chambers of guilty delight,
  There walk the spectres of guilty fear,
And soft low voices, that float through the night,
  Are whispering sin in the helpless ear.

Dear maid, in thy girlhood's opening flower,
  Scarce weaned from the love of childish play!
The tears on whose cheeks are but the shower
  That freshens the blooms of early May!

Thine eyes are closed, and over thy brow
  Pass thoughtful shadows and joyous gleams,
And I know, by thy moving lips, that now
  Thy spirit strays in the Land of Dreams.

Light-hearted maiden, oh, heed thy feet!
  Oh keep where that beam of Paradise falls:
And only wander where thou mayst meet
  The blessed ones from its shining walls!

So shalt thou come from the Land of Dreams,
  With love and peace to this world of strife:
And the light which over that border streams
  Shall lie on the path of thy daily life.

"O MOTHER OF A MIGHTY RACE."

Written after a journey to Europe, and at a time when there was danger of war with England over the question of the northwestern boundary.

O MOTHER of a mighty race,
Yet lovely in thy youthful grace!
The elder dames, thy haughty peers,
Admire and hate thy blooming years.
With words of shame
And taunts of scorn they join thy name.

For on thy cheeks the glow is spread
That tints thy morning hills with red;
Thy step — the wild-deer's rustling feet
Within thy woods are not more fleet;
Thy hopeful eye
Is bright as thine own sunny sky.

Ay, let them rail — those haughty ones,
While safe thou dwellest with thy sons.
They do not know how loved thou art,
How many a fond and fearless heart
Would rise to throw
Its life between thee and the foe.

They know not, in their hate and pride,
What virtues with thy children bide;
How true, how good, thy graceful maids
Make bright, like flowers, the valley-shades;
What generous men
Spring, like thine oaks, by hill and glen;—

What cordial welcomes greet the guest
By thy lone rivers of the West;
How faith is kept, and truth revered,
And man is loved, and God is feared,
In woodland homes,
And where the ocean border foams.

There 's freedom at thy gates and rest
For Earth's down-trodden and oppressed,
A shelter for the hunted head,
For the starved laborer toil and bread.
Power at thy bounds,
Stops and calls back his baffled hounds.

O fair young mother! on thy brow
Shall sit a nobler grace than now.
Deep in the brightness of the skies
The thronging years in glory rise,
And, as they fleet,
Drop strength and riches at thy feet.

Thine eye, with every coming hour,
Shall brighten, and thy form shall tower;
And when thy sisters, elder born,
Would brand thy name with words of scorn,
Before thine eye,
Upon their lips the taunt shall die.

OUR COUNTRY'S CALL.

Written in September, 1861.

LAY down the axe; fling by the spade;
Leave in its track the toiling plough;

The rifle and the bayonet-blade
  For arms like yours were fitter now;
And let the hands that ply the pen
  Quit the light task, and learn to wield
The horseman's crooked brand, and rein
  The charger on the battle-field.

Our country calls; away! away!
  To where the blood-stream blots the green.
Strike to defend the gentlest sway
  That Time in all his course has seen.
See, from a thousand coverts — see,
  Spring the armed foes that haunt her track;
They rush to smite her down, and we
  Must beat the banded traitors back.

Ho! sturdy as the oaks ye cleave,
  And moved as soon to fear and flight,
Men of the glade and forest! leave
  Your woodcraft for the field of fight.
The arms that wield the axe must pour
  An iron tempest on the foe;
His serried ranks shall reel before
  The arm that lays the panther low.

And ye, who breast the mountain-storm
  By grassy steep or highland lake,
Come, for the land ye love, to form
  A bulwark that no foe can break.
Stand, like your own gray cliffs that mock
  The whirlwind, stand in her defence;
The blast as soon shall move the rock
  As rushing squadrons bear ye thence.

And ye, whose homes are by her grand
  Swift rivers, rising far away,
Come from the depth of her green land,
  As mighty in your march as they;
As terrible as when the rains
  Have swelled them over bank and bourne,
With sudden floods to drown the plains
  And sweep along the woods uptorn.

And ye, who throng, beside the deep,
  Her ports and hamlets of the strand,
In number like the waves that leap
  On his long-murmuring marge of sand—
Come like that deep, when, o'er his brim,
  He rises, all his floods to pour,
And flings the proudest barks that swim,
  A helpless wreck, against the shore!

Few, few were they whose swords of old
  Won the fair land in which we dwell;
But we are many, we who hold
  The grim resolve to guard it well.
Strike, for that broad and goodly land,
  Blow after blow, till men shall see
That Might and Right move hand in hand,
  And glorious must their triumph be!

THE RETURN OF THE BIRDS.

Written in March, 1864.

I HEAR, from many a little throat,
  A warble interrupted long;
I hear the robin's flute-like note,
  The bluebird's slenderer song.

Brown meadows and the russet hill,
  Not yet the haunt of grazing herds,
And thickets by the glimmering rill,
  Are all alive with birds.

O choir of spring, why come so soon?
  On leafless grove and herbless lawn
Warm lie the yellow beams of moon;
  Yet winter is not gone.

For frost shall sheet the pools again;
  Again the blustering East shall blow —
Whirl a white tempest through the glen,
  And load the pines with snow.

Yet, haply, from the region where,
  Waked by an earlier spring than here,
The blossomed wild-plum scents the air,
  Ye come in haste and fear.

For there is heard the bugle-blast,
  The booming gun, the jarring drum,
And on their chargers, spurring fast,
  Armed warriors go and come.

There mighty hosts have pitched the camp
  In valleys that were yours till then,
And Earth has shuddered to the tramp
  Of half a million men!

In groves where once ye used to sing,
  In orchards where ye had your birth,
A thousand glittering axes swing
  To smite the trees to earth.

Ye love the fields by ploughmen trod;
But there, when sprouts the beechen spray,
The soldier only breaks the sod
To hide the slain away.

Stay, then, beneath our ruder sky;
Heed not the storm-clouds rising black,
Nor yelling winds that with them fly;
Nor let them fright you back, —

Back to the stifling battle-cloud,
To burning towns that blot the day,
And trains of mounting dust that shroud
The armies on their way.

Stay, for a tint of green shall creep
Soon o'er the orchard's grassy floor,
And from its bed the crocus peep,
Beside the housewife's door.

Here build, and dread no harsher sound,
To scare you from the sheltering tree,
Than winds that stir the branches round,
And murmur of the bee.

And we will pray that, ere again
The flowers of autumn bloom and die,
Our generals and their strong-armed men
May lay their weapons by.

Then may ye warble, unafraid,
Where hands, that wear the fetter now,
Free as your wings shall ply the spade,
And guide the peaceful plough.

Then, as our conquering hosts return,
What shouts of jubilee shall break
From placid vale and mountain stern,
And shore of mighty lake!

And midland plain and ocean-strand
Shall thunder: "Glory to the brave,
Peace to the torn and bleeding land,
And freedom to the slave!"

ABRAHAM LINCOLN.

Written by request, when the funeral procession of the martyred President passed through the streets of New York.

OH, slow to smite and swift to spare,
Gentle and merciful and just!
Who, in the fear of God, didst bear
The sword of power, a nation's trust!

In sorrow by thy bier we stand,
Amid the awe that hushes all,
And speak the anguish of a land
That shook with horror at thy fall.

Thy task is done; the bond are free:
We bear thee to an honored grave,
Whose proudest monument shall be
The broken fetters of the slave.

Pure was thy life; its bloody close
Hath placed thee with the sons of light,
Among the noble host of those
Who perished in the cause of Right.

THE SONG OF THE SOWER.

I.

THE maples redden in the sun;
  In autumn gold the beeches stand;
Rest, faithful plough, thy work is done
  Upon the teeming land.
Bordered with trees whose gay leaves fly
On every breath that sweeps the sky,
The fresh dark acres furrowed lie,
  And ask the sower's hand.
Loose the tired steer and let him go
To pasture where the gentians blow.
And we, who till the grateful ground,
Fling we the golden shower around.

II.

Fling wide the generous grain; we fling
O'er the dark mould the green of spring.
For thick the emerald blades shall grow,
When first the March winds melt the snow,
And to the sleeping flowers, below,
    The early bluebirds sing.
Fling wide the grain; we give the fields
  The ears that nod in summer's gale,
The shining stems that summer gilds,
  The harvest that o'erflows the vale,
And swells, an amber sea, between
The full-leaved woods, its shores of green.
Hark! from the murmuring clods I hear
Glad voices of the coming year;
The song of him who binds the grain,
The shout of those that load the wain,

And from the distant grange there comes
The clatter of the thresher's flail,
And steadily the millstone hums
Down in the willowy vale.

III.

Fling wide the golden shower; we trust
The strength of armies to the dust.
This peaceful lea may haply yield
Its harvest for the tented field.
Ha! feel ye not your fingers thrill,
As o'er them, in the yellow grains,
Glide the warm drops of blood that fill,
For mortal strife, the warrior's veins;
Such as, on Solferino's day,
Slaked the brown sand and flowed away —
Flowed till the herds, on Mincio's brink,
Snuffed the red stream and feared to drink; —
Blood that in deeper pools shall lie,
On the sad earth, as time grows gray,
When men by deadlier arts shall die,
And deeper darkness blot the sky
Above the thundering fray;
And realms, that hear the battle-cry,
Shall sicken with dismay;
And chieftains to the war shall lead
Whole nations, with the tempest's speed,
To perish in a day; —
Till man, by love and mercy taught,
Shall rue the wreck his fury wrought,
And lay the sword away!
Oh strew, with pausing, shuddering hand,
The seed upon the helpless land,
As if, at every step, ye cast
The pelting hail and riving blast.

IV.

Nay, strew, with free and joyous sweep,
  The seed upon the expecting soil;
For hence the plenteous year shall heap
  The garners of the men who toil.
Strew the bright seed for those who tear
The matted sward with spade and share,
And those whose sounding axes gleam
Beside the lonely forest-stream,
    Till its broad banks lie bare;
And him who breaks the quarry-ledge,
  With hammer-blows, plied quick and strong,
And him who, with the steady sledge,
  Smites the shrill anvil all day long.
Sprinkle the furrow's even trace
  For those whose toiling hands uprear
The roof-trees of our swarming race,
  By grove and plain, by stream and mere;
Who forth, from crowded city, lead
  The lengthening street, and overlay
Green orchard-plot and grassy mead
  With pavement of the murmuring way.
Cast, with full hands the harvest cast,
For the brave men that climb the mast,
When to the billow and the blast
  It swings and stoops, with fearful strain,
And bind the fluttering mainsail fast,
  Till the tossed bark shall sit, again,
  Safe as a sea-bird on the main.

V.

Fling wide the grain for those who throw
The clanking shuttle to and fro,
In the long row of humming rooms,

And into ponderous masses wind
The web that, from a thousand looms,
Comes forth to clothe mankind.
Strew, with free sweep, the grain for them,
By whom the busy thread
Along the garment's even hem
And winding seam is led;
A pallid sisterhood, that keep
The lonely lamp alight,
In strife with weariness and sleep,
Beyond the middle night.
Large part be theirs in what the year
Shall ripen for the reaper here.

VI.

Still, strew, with joyous hand, the wheat
On the soft mould beneath our feet,
For even now I seem
To hear a sound that lightly rings
From murmuring harp and viol's strings,
As in a summer dream.
The welcome of the wedding-guest,
The bridegroom's look of bashful pride,
The faint smile of the pallid bride,
And bridemaid's blush at matron's jest,
And dance and song and generous dower,
Are in the shining grains we shower.

VII.

Scatter the wheat for shipwrecked men,
Who, hunger-worn, rejoice again
In the sweet safety of the shore,
And wanderers, lost in woodlands drear,
Whose pulses bound with joy to hear

The herd's light bell once more.
Freely the golden spray be shed
For him whose heart, when night comes down
On the close alleys of the town,
Is faint for lack of bread.
In chill roof-chambers, bleak and bare,
Or the damp cellar's stifling air,
She who now sees, in mute despair,
Her children pine for food,
Shall feel the dews of gladness start
To lids long tearless, and shall part
The sweet loaf with a grateful heart,
Among her thin pale brood.
Dear, kindly Earth, whose breast we till!
Oh, for thy famished children, fill,
Where'er the sower walks,
Fill the rich ears that shade the mould
With grain for grain, a hundredfold,
To bend the sturdy stalks.

VIII.

Strew silently the fruitful seed,
As softly o'er the tilth ye tread,
For hands that delicately knead
The consecrated bread —
The mystic loaf that crowns the board,
When, round the table of their Lord,
Within a thousand temples set,
In memory of the bitter death
Of Him who taught at Nazareth,
His followers are met,
And thoughtful eyes with tears are wet,
As of the Holy One they think,
The glory of whose rising yet
Makes bright the grave's mysterious brink.

IX.

Brethren, the sower's task is done.
The seed is in its winter bed.
Now let the dark-brown mould be spread,
To hide it from the sun,
And leave it to the kindly care
Of the still earth and brooding air,
As when the mother, from her breast,
Lays the hushed babe apart to rest,
And shades its eyes, and waits to see
How sweet its waking smile will be.
The tempest now may smite, the sleet
All night on the drowned furrow beat,
And winds that, from the cloudy hold.
Of winter breathe the bitter cold,
Stiffen to stone the mellow mould,
Yet safe shall lie the wheat;
Till, out of heaven's unmeasured blue,
Shall walk again the genial year,
To wake with warmth and nurse with dew
The germs we lay to slumber here.

X.

Oh blessed harvest yet to be!
Abide thou with the Love that keeps,
In its warm bosom, tenderly,
The Life which wakes and that which sleeps.
The Love that leads the willing spheres
Along the unending track of years,
And watches o'er the sparrow's nest,
Shall brood above thy winter rest,
And raise thee from the dust, to hold
Light whisperings with the winds of May,
And fill thy spikes with living gold,

From summer's yellow ray;
Then, as thy garners give thee forth,
On what glad errands shalt thou go,
Wherever, o'er the waiting earth,
Roads wind and rivers flow!
The ancient East shall welcome thee
To mighty marts beyond the sea,
And they who dwell where palm-groves sound
To summer winds the whole year round,
Shall watch, in gladness, from the shore,
The sails that bring thy glistening store.

THE FLOOD OF YEARS.

Written in the poet's eighty-third year.

A MIGHTY Hand, from an exhaustless Urn,
Pours forth the never-ending Flood of Years,
Among the nations. How the rushing waves
Bear all before them! On their foremost edge,
And there alone, is Life. The Present there
Tosses and foams, and fills the air with roar
Of mingled noises. There are they who toil,
And they who strive, and they who feast, and they
Who hurry to and fro. The sturdy swain —
Woodman and delver with the spade — is there,
And busy artisan beside his bench,
And pallid student with his written roll.
A moment on the mounting billow seen,
The flood sweeps over them and they are gone.
There groups of revellers, whose brows are twined
With roses, ride the topmost swell awhile,
And as they raise their flowing cups and touch
The clinking brim to brim, are whirled beneath

The waves and disappear. I hear the jar
Of beaten drums, and thunders that break forth
From cannon, where the advancing billow sends
Up to the sight long files of armèd men,
That hurry to the charge through flame and smoke.
The torrent bears them under, whelmed and hid
Slayer and slain, in heaps of bloody foam.
Down go the steed and rider, the plumed chief
Sinks with his followers; the head that wears
The imperial diadem goes down beside
The felon's with cropped ear and branded cheek.
A funeral-train — the torrent sweeps away
Bearers and bier and mourners. By the bed
Of one who dies men gather sorrowing,
And women weep aloud; the flood rolls on;
The wail is stifled and the sobbing group
Borne under. Hark to that shrill, sudden shout,
The cry of an applauding multitude,
Swayed by some loud-voiced orator who wields
The living mass as if he were its soul!
The waters choke the shout and all is still.
Lo! next a kneeling crowd, and one who spreads
The hands in prayer — the engulfing wave o'ertakes
And swallows them and him. A sculptor wields
The chisel, and the stricken marble grows
To beauty; at his easel, eager-eyed,
A painter stands, and sunshine at his touch
Gathers upon his canvas, and life glows;
A poet, as he paces to and fro,
Murmurs his sounding lines. Awhile they ride
The advancing billow, till its tossing crest
Strikes them and flings them under, while their tasks
Are yet unfinished. See a mother smile
On her young babe that smiles to her again;

The torrent wrests it from her arms; she shrieks
And weeps, and midst her tears is carried down.
A beam like that of moonlight turns the spray
To glistening pearls; two lovers, hand in hand,
Rise on the billowy swell and fondly look
Into each other's eyes. The rushing flood
Flings them apart: the youth goes down; the maid
With hands outstretched in vain, and streaming eyes,
Waits for the next high wave to follow him.
An aged man succeeds; his bending form
Sinks slowly. Mingling with the sullen stream
Gleam the white locks, and then are seen no more.
  Lo! wider grows the stream — a sea-like flood
Saps earth's walled cities; massive palaces
Crumble before it; fortresses and towers
Dissolve in the swift waters; populous realms
Swept by the torrent see their ancient tribes
Engulfed and lost; their very languages
Stifled, and never to be uttered more.
  I pause and turn my eyes, and looking back
Where that tumultuous flood has been, I see
The silent ocean of the Past, a waste
Of waters weltering over graves, its shores
Strewn with the wreck of fleets where mast and hull
Drop away piecemeal; battlemented walls
Frown idly, green with moss, and temples stand
Unroofed, forsaken by the worshipper.
There lie memorial stones, whence time has gnawed
The graven legends, thrones of kings o'erturned,
The broken altars of forgotten gods,
Foundations of old cities and long streets
Where never fall of human foot is heard,
On all the desolate pavement. I behold
Dim glimmerings of lost jewels, far within

The sleeping waters, diamond, sardonyx,
Ruby and topaz, pearl and chrysolite,
Once glittering at the banquet on fair brows
That long ago were dust, and all around
Strewn on the surface of that silent sea
Are withering bridal wreaths, and glossy locks
Shorn from dear brows, by loving hands, and scrolls
O'er written, haply with fond words of love
And vows of friendship, and fair pages flung
Fresh from the printer's engine. There they lie
A moment, and then sink away from sight.
I look, and the quick tears are in my eyes,
For I behold in every one of these
A blighted hope, a separate history
Of human sorrows, telling of dear ties
Suddenly broken, dreams of happiness
Dissolved in air, and happy days too brief
That sorrowfully ended, and I think
How painfully must the poor heart have beat
In bosoms without number, as the blow
Was struck that slew their hope and broke their peace.
Sadly I turn and look before, where yet
The Flood must pass, and I behold a mist
Where swarm dissolving forms, the brood of Hope,
Divinely fair, that rest on banks of flowers,
Or wander among rainbows, fading soon
And reappearing, haply giving place
To forms of grisly aspect such as Fear
Shapes from the idle air — where serpents lift
The head to strike, and skeletons stretch forth
The bony arm in menace. Further on
A belt of darkness seems to bar the way
Long, low, and distant, where the Life to come

Touches the Life that is. The Flood of Years
Rolls toward it near and nearer. It must pass
That dismal barrier. What is there beyond?
Hear what the wise and good have said. Beyond
That belt of darkness, still the Years roll on
More gently, but with not less mighty sweep.
They gather up again and softly bear
All the sweet lives that late were overwhelmed
And lost to sight, all that in them was good,
Noble, and truly great, and worthy of love —
The lives of infants and ingenuous youths,
Sages and saintly women who have made
Their households happy; all are raised and borne
By that great current in its onward sweep,
Wandering and rippling with caressing waves
Around green islands with the breath
Of flowers that never wither. So they pass
From stage to stage along the shining course
Of that bright river, broadening like a sea.
As its smooth eddies curl along their way
They bring old friends together; hands are clasped
In joy unspeakable; the mother's arms
Again are folded round the child she loved
And lost. Old sorrows are forgotten now,
Or but remembered to make sweet the hour
That overpays them; wounded hearts that bled
Or broke are healed forever. In the room
Of this grief-shadowed present, there shall be
A Present in whose reign no grief shall gnaw
The heart, and never shall a tender tie
Be broken; in whose reign the eternal Change
That waits on growth and action shall proceed
With everlasting Concord hand in hand.

THANATOPSIS.

Written in the poet's eighteenth year.

To him who in the love of Nature holds
Communion with her visible forms, she speaks
A various language; for his gayer hours
She has a voice of gladness, and a smile
And eloquence of beauty, and she glides
Into his darker musings, with a mild
And healing sympathy, that steals away
Their sharpness, ere he is aware. When thoughts
Of the last bitter hour come like a blight
Over thy spirit, and sad images
Of the stern agony, and shroud, and pall,
And breathless darkness, and the narrow house,
Make thee to shudder, and grow sick at heart; —
Go forth, under the open sky, and list
To Nature's teachings, while from all around —
Earth and her waters, and the depths of air —
Comes a still voice —

Yet a few days, and thee
The all-beholding sun shall see no more
In all his course; nor yet in the cold ground,
Where thy pale form was laid, with many tears,
Nor in the embrace of ocean, shall exist
Thy image. Earth, that nourished thee, shall claim
Thy growth, to be resolved to earth again,
And, lost each human trace, surrendering up
Thine individual being, shalt thou go
To mix forever with the elements,
To be a brother to the insensible rock
And to the sluggish clod, which the rude swain

Turns with his share, and treads upon. The oak
Shall send his roots abroad, and pierce thy mould.

Yet not to thine eternal resting-place
Shalt thou retire alone, nor couldst thou wish
Couch more magnificent. Thou shalt lie down
With patriarchs of the infant world — with kings,
The powerful of the earth — the wise, the good,
Fair forms, and hoary seers of ages past,
All in one mighty sepulchre. The hills
Rock-ribbed and ancient as the sun, — the vales
Stretching in pensive quietness between;
The venerable woods — rivers that move
In majesty, and the complaining brooks
That make the meadows green; and, poured round all,
Old Ocean's gray and melancholy waste, —
Are but the solemn decorations all
Of the great tomb of man. The golden sun,
The planets, all the infinite host of heaven,
Are shining on the sad abodes of death,
Through the still lapse of ages. All that tread
The globe are but a handful to the tribes
That slumber in its bosom. — Take the wings
Of morning, pierce the Barcan wilderness,
Or lose thyself in the continuous woods
Where rolls the Oregon, and hears no sound,
Save his own dashings — yet the dead are there:
And millions in those solitudes, since first
The flight of years began, have laid them down
In their last sleep — the dead reign there alone.
So shalt thou rest, and what if thou withdraw
In silence from the living, and no friend
Take note of thy departure? All that breathe

Will share thy destiny, The gay will laugh
When thou art gone, the solemn brood of care
Plod on, and each one as before will chase
His favorite phantom; yet all these shall leave
Their mirth and their employments, and shall come
And make their bed with thee. As the long train
Of ages glides away, the sons of men,
The youth in life's fresh spring, and he who goes
In the full strength of years, matron and maid,
The speechless babe, and the gray-headed man —
Shall one by one be gathered to thy side,
By those who in their turn shall follow them.

So live, that when thy summons comes to join
The innumerable caravan, which moves
To that mysterious realm, where each shall take
His chamber in the silent halls of death,
Thou go not, like the quarry-slave at night,
Scourged to his dungeon, but, sustained and soothed
By an unfaltering trust, approach thy grave
Like one who wraps the drapery of his couch
About him, and lies down to pleasant dreams.